For the Duration

To
Tony and Anne

Best Wishes

Gordon
Nisbett
January 1997

For the Duration

The Journal of a Conscript
1941 to 1946

Gordon Nisbett

The Pentland Press Limited
Edinburgh • Cambridge • Durham • USA

First published in 1996 by
The Pentland Press Ltd.
1 Hutton Close
South Church
Bishop Auckland
Durham

British Library Cataloguing in Publication Data.
A catalogue record for this book is available
from the British Library.

ISBN 1 85821 346 0

Typeset by CBS, Felixstowe, Suffolk
Printed and bound by Antony Rowe Ltd., Chippenham

Dedicated to
the Officers and men of the
1st Reconnaissance Regiment
1941-1946

To suffer passes away,
But to have suffered never passes.
The gain of experience
will be ours for ever.

French Proverb translated

CONTENTS

FOREWORD

by Brig. (Retd) EW Anstey OBE (Late of the Reconnaissance Corps
and The Royal Tank Regiment)

It is a great privilege to have been invited to contribute a Foreword to
Gordon Nisbett's volume of reminiscence. This is more so as I served
in 1st Reconnaissance Regiment from almost the time of its formation
until its end in 1946; being amongst the first officers to be
commissioned directly to the First. The greater part of Gordon's
narrative concerns his time with his Regiment and in particular with
'C' Squadron. For much of this time I was indeed the Adjutant.

The Reconnaissance Corps was formed following Dunkirk in
order to release the Cavalry Regiments (which had hitherto provided
the reconnaissance element of the infantry divisions) to man the
rapidly increasing number of tank regiments. It was thought, quite
rightly, that their predominantly regular element would convert
more readily to the heavy armoured role. As a result the Reconnaissance
Corps was formed from widely disparate sources of manpower and
with a variety of *ad hoc* equipment as Gordon's narrative makes clear.

At the end of the war our hopes were that the Corps would find a
place in the regular Order of Battle but it was not to be and we were
disbanded, handing back our responsibilities to the infantry divisions,
to the same cavalry we had once replaced.

One of the consequences of this arrangement was that the Corps
had no regular base to enshrine its newly created traditions (nor
indeed its memories) although many Reconnaissance Regiments have
maintained their Comrades Associations and Memorials (as the First
has done to this day in Stamford in Lincolnshire where it was formed
in January 1941).

A particular regrettable aspect is that there have been few Regimental histories (although Jeremy Taylor's *His Band of Brothers* was an early and gallant attempt to cover the story of the Corps as a whole). I am sure Gordon would disclaim it but he has in fact produced a very close approximation to such a history for the First. For this reason amongst others, I applaud his book.

Of course he has been concerned to relate the dramatic life of the ordinary trooper. This he has done in comprehensive fashion, recalling what it was like to face danger and discomfort day by day in two of the most demanding theatres in which the British Army fought in 1939-45. At the same time readers will find the background, the tactical and strategic considerations and the decisions both good and indifferent sketched in which lucidity and care and, for a trooper, with remarkable sympathy and understanding.

Moreover in one of his concluding chapters he has summarized the view of what it was all about from the point of view of a soldier in the carrier or armoured car or, as often as not, on foot in a slit trench. He is right to emphasize the time we spent as auxiliary (or even primary) infantry as befitted a regiment equipped and trained to cover the essentials of both infantry and armoured operations.

It may be appropriate however to emphasize that the First engaged with great élan in three classic reconnaissance roles although the first two are proper examples of reconnaissance in the pursuit. First the advance from Medjez el Bab to Tunis on the left flank of 1st Division to the outskirts of Bizerta. Second, the break out from Anzio to Rome when the Regiment, having been prevented for political reasons from entering the city, drove on over the Tiber almost to Civitavecchia before being recalled (with some difficulty). Finally the drive down the Arno from Pontassieve to Florence and northward until we were emeshed in the Gothic Line. None who took part will forget the excitement and exuberance of these typical and effective reconnaissance actions.

But Gordon has got it all down and has caught the Regimental spirit exactly. I, for one, am most grateful to him for having written *For the Duration* and commend it to all his readers. The old will remember what he is writing about and I expect the young will marvel at how much was endured whilst the comrades who fell and who are recorded in our Memorial in All Saints Church, Stamford, will have at last something of an epitaph to say how it was they gave their lives.

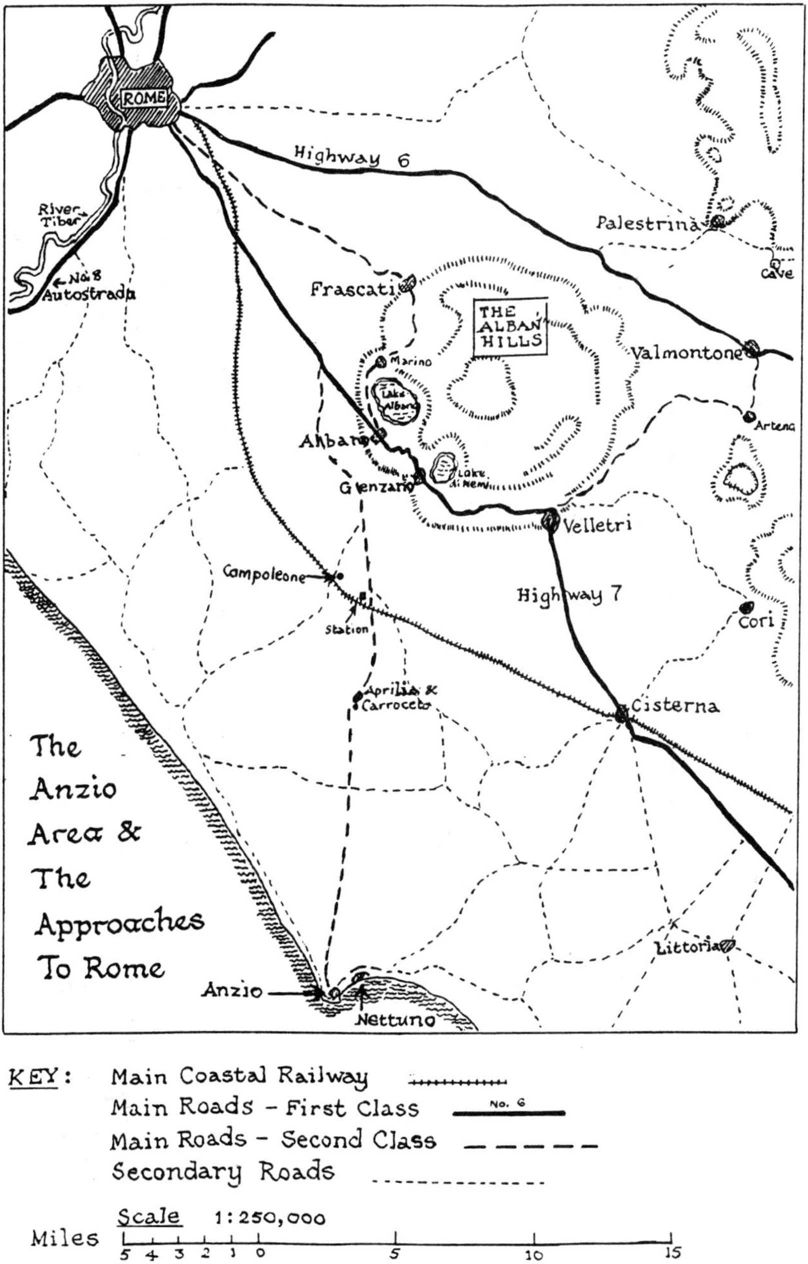

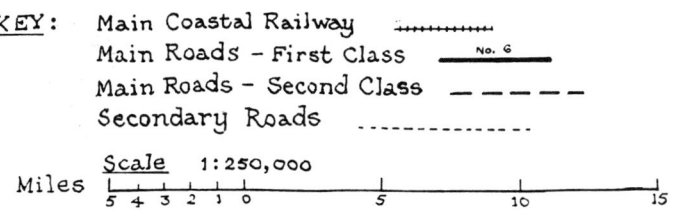

ROME

River Tiber

← No 8 Autostrada

Highway 6

Palestrina

Cave

Frascati

THE ALBAN HILLS

Valmontone

Marino

Lake Albano

Artena

Albano

Lake di Nemi

Genzano

Velletri

Campoleone

Highway 7

Cori

Station

Aprilia & Carroceto

Cisterna

The Anzio Area & The Approaches To Rome

Littoria

Anzio →

Nettuno

KEY: Main Coastal Railway ┄┄┄┄┄┄

Main Roads – First Class   ━━━ No. 6

Main Roads – Second Class ─ ─ ─ ─

Secondary Roads ┈┈┈┈┈┈┈

Scale   1:250,000

Miles 5 4 3 2 1 0   5   10   15

ORGANISATION OF A RECONNAISSANCE REGIMENT

Regimental Headquarters

- Headquarters Squadron
- Reconnaissance Squadron
- Reconnaissance Squadron
- Reconnaissance Squadron

Squadron Headquarters
- Signal Troop
- Mortar Troop (Six 3-inch Mortars)
- Anti-Tank Troop
  - Troop
  - Troop
  - Battery Headquarters
  (Four 6-pounder Anti-tank Guns)
- Administrative Troop

Squadron Headquarters
- Scout Troop
- Scout Troop
- Scout Troop
- Assault Troop

Troop Headquarters
- Reconnaissance Section (Two Armoured Cars, Two Light Reconnaissance Cars)
- Bren Carrier Section
- Carrier Section (Three Bren Carriers)

Troop Headquarters
- Section
- Section
- Section
- Section

Corporal
Lance Corporal
Five Troopers
(Driver in charge of 15-cwt. truck)

One

Prelude

I was born in the summer of 1922, the second of four children. At the time of my birth, my father was a builder of transformers in the Ferranti Works at Hollinwood, near Oldham. My mother was the eldest of eight children, the daughter of a clerk in the office of Colliers, Iron Founders in Macclesfield. In 1909, she was clever enough to be the only girl, in the little town of Congleton, to pass the examination for entrance into the prestigious Macclesfield High School for Girls. Alas, distance and poverty, the blight of her time, denied her the privilege. Later, when she married, she imparted her knowledge and wisdom to my three sisters and myself. Regularly at eventide, after daily chores, she saved a magical hour for the telling of stories which ended in prayers and in the night-lighted climb of the stairs to bed. The outcome of her endeavours was that I became a fluent and an avid reader by the time I was five years old.

As I grew, I became more shy, more reserved and more sensitive. More than that, an upbringing in a stable and staunchly Christian environment had endowed me with a developing conscience and a degree of compassion. In the forming of these traits, my parents had a considerable role. On hindsight, my father was insecure, masking his discomfort by being severe, domineering and possessive of his children. But he was not devoid of feelings and affection for us.

We were children of the Thirties, a decade of overwhelming recession and poverty which affected adversely both my father's nature and mine. No longer travelling to Hollinwood, my father had found work in the silk industry of Macclesfield, only to endure a slump in silk manufacturing that brought a long period in which he was constantly in and out of employment. He became deeply depressed and ashamed of his predicament. Like many other 'laid-off' men he blamed himself for being out of work. I, in empathy, absorbed his melancholy and shame which I felt deeply in the presence of those of my peers whose fathers did not have to stand in long, daily queues at the Labour Exchange. Throughout those hard times, my mother's hopeful Christian stance sustained me. The difference between right and wrong was made abundantly clear. Furthermore, by her example, I had become compassionate. I remember that, poor as we were, she passed on our worn clothing and shoes to a larger family even poorer than her own.

My growing compassion is revealed in an incident of my childhood which I can not erase from my memory. Often I would roam through a well-loved stretch of hilly and beautiful countryside known as The Hollins. Towards its end was Noah's Hill, a rounded mound with its lower slopes clad in burgeoning bracken. Above, closer to the summit, stretched a band of rough, upland grass which gave way to a small, rocky outcrop which marked the peak.

Because of the presence of a skylark which hovered and sang above the slopes and then dropped like a stone, I decided to climb through the bracken to seek its nest. As I began my search in the upland grass I disturbed the sitting bird. The grounded lark rose with a cry of alarm. At that moment, to my horror, I had clumsily trodden underfoot its nest and the brood of tiny skylarks. Their dying squeaks smote me like a savage blow. I sat down by the ruined nest and dead nestlings. The distraught mother had returned circling above with heart-rending cries which penetrated deep into my being. Sharing her grief I wept. When at last she flew away, I moved down the hillside disconsolate and saddened but with a lasting reverence for life.

As I grew older still, so the war clouds began to gather and loom, casting an ominous shadow over my youth. In Europe there was blatant annexation of territory by Germany. In Africa, Italy was expanding her empire while, in Britain, words of appeasement took precedence over courageous action against the aggressors. Then, at a late hour Britain began to arm and make ready for war.

My thoughts became concerned with the possibility of my being conscripted to serve in the armed forces. Already, in early

1939, the Government had called up the Militia, a group of men who were only five years older than myself. Plans were being made for further conscription.

Then, in September, war was declared. Zealously, with most of my friends, I wanted to serve in the armed forces but, with self recognition of my physical and mental dispositions, I seemed wholly unsuited for warfare. I became haunted by fears of rejection. To add to my apprehension, my father expressed the view that I would never serve in the armed forces, his misgivings being based only on my severe shortsightedness. But, I had other physical defects of which I was well aware: in my socks, I was just 5'3½" tall, heredity had endowed me with bandy legs, and I was born with a birthmark on my chin which had helped make me more sensitive. More than that, I was red–green colour blind, a defect which ruled out any service in the Royal Air Force or in the Royal Navy. All my hopes were founded on my being accepted as a non-combatant in the Army.

In 1940, when I was eighteen years old, I registered for military service. In the spring of 1941, with trepidation, I presented myself for medical examination at the former Pendlebury Orphanage, on Lancashire Hill, in Stockport. There I joined a queue of men awaiting the dreaded eyesight test. With my father's premonition in mind, apprehensively, I confronted the triangle of graduating letters which started with a largest one at the top. Without spectacles my performance was dismal: I succeeded in reading only the three largest letters at the top of the pyramid.

So, as my spirits lowered, my fear of rejection grew. With my glasses restored, I was asked to read again. This time I made progress down to the penultimate line. Then, quickly, the examination was over. I left the room and its noncommittal examiner.

Later, stripped to the waist, I joined a line of half-naked young men, each of us waiting to pass through a series of open-ended cubicles, each manned by an examining doctor. Like raw factory material, we waited to be processed by doctors who, in demeanour, acted like bored operatives on routine factory work. With deadpan faces they gave orders such as,

'Breathe in!' 'Breathe out!'

'Bend over!' 'Touch your toes!'

'Cough!' 'Sit down!' 'Cross your legs!'
'Urinate into this!'
Between these commands, our chests and backs were finger
tapped, our heartbeats measured, our reflexes tested and our
orifices intimately examined. Eventually, at the end of the
production line, we dressed to await the verdict of the Assessing
Officer, a sort of quality controller with power to reject flawed
products. I came before him.
'Are you feeling well?' he asked.
In my state of anxiety, this remark raised fresh doubts and fears
of undiscovered illnesses but, with haste, I affirmed that I was
well. His next action changed my despondency into elation when,
in bright red ink, he wrote A1 on the card he gave to me. Now it
seemed that I would be called to serve in His Majesty's Army. The
flaws in my physical make-up had been overlooked. It seemed that
stringent standards of physical fitness had been shelved in order
to rebuild the Army, depleted after the fall of France.
It was some months after my acceptance when the brown
envelope arrived. I remember plainly its contents and the opening
sentence of my summons. It read,

'On Thursday, 23 October 1941, you will report to the
Infantry Training Centre (Reconnaissance Training Centre),
Halleaths Camp, Lochmaben, Dumfriesshire, Scotland.'

A single travel warrant accompanied the order. There was
information concerned with my time of arrival at Lockerbie
station as well as instructions to bring an empty suitcase in which
to return my civilian clothing. I was puzzled by the bracketed
words, Reconnaissance Training Centre. I sought information but
no one seemed to know of such a unit. My dictionary explained
the word reconnoitre - to try to learn position and condition or
strategic features of the enemy. I began to consider that I - the
myopic, undersized conscript - would be trained as a front line
soldier. I was to know my fortune soon enough.
On the day of my leaving home, I travelled by northbound
express from Macclesfield. Others boarded the train with me. All
were hatless, suited, fresh faced youths of nineteen years, bearing
their tell-tale suitcases and already showing a uniformity of dress

4

which the Army was about to demand.

As the express train steamed northwards, the carriages began to fill with conscripts, one or two regulars returning from leave and a few travelling civilians. At Carlisle came the divide. Half the conscripts detrained. Their destination: Hadrian's Camp and service in the Royal Artillery.

At Lockerbie station we alighted, a leaderless, shuffling draft, at once aware that we had crossed the border. On a deserted platform an imposing figure awaited: a ruddy-faced Scotsman, resplendent in kilt and glengarry; his smart, khaki tunic adorned with gleaming, brass buttons; a colourful, red sash stretching obliquely from shoulder to waist. He introduced himself as Corporal McLean, late of the Highland Light Infantry. We gathered round him for a roll call, our names being pronounced with a strong, Glaswegian burr. Then, like sheep we trailed from the station platform into the town square. Outside the gate stood several Bedford trucks into which we clambered for the journey to Halleaths Camp. Aboard, with standing room only, and gripping our cases, we clung with one hand to the metal framework of the canvas cover, jolting and swaying like drunken men.

On arrival at our destination we were ill prepared for what we saw. The camp had been occupied only since January of 1941. It was a dismal sight under the lowering, black rain clouds of the late October day. Recently, there had been heavy rains so that the black Nissen huts seemed to wallow like humpbacked whales in a sea of mud. Roads and pathways were barely visible under a skimming of liquid mud. As we dropped down from the truck, we saw a lone bedraggled figure; a general duties soldier wearing a long mud-spattered greatcoat and leaning dismally on his stiff, hard-bristled brush. Overwhelmed by the immensity of his sweeping task, he managed a head shaking greeting, ironically uttering the words, 'You lucky people!'

Undismayed by the irony, I was taken to be registered and became 10600871 Private Nisbett G. of Number 2 Squad, Number 2 Recruit Company. Along with the rest of the squad I was fed and then, in failing light, we filled empty palliasses and pillows with straw, collected three blankets each and, loaded like Sherpas, clumsily traversed the slippery ground until we arrived at our quarters, one of a line of Nissen huts.

Inside, the décor and furnishings could not have been more simplistic. The dimly lit hut had an inner, corrugated steel skin which had been whitewashed in an attempt to lighten the gloom. Already in place, on the concrete floor, on either side of the central aisle were rows of the most primitive beds. Each bed being three long planks of roughly planed wood supported by two triangular legs of steel. Two feet of space separated each bed from the next. Half way down the aisle, a lighted cast-iron stove was burning the evening's ration of coke.

The only other observable facility was an oversized bucket which had a permanent place outside the door. We learned quickly that it was for our convenience and relief at night. Soon, we endowed it with the title of 'piss' bucket. On each successive morning it was never less than brimful and had to be carried half a mile to the emptying point by two recruits appointed for each day.

The first night was unforgettable. Deprived of chairs and still in civilian clothing, we sat, apprehensively, on beds adjacent to the comforting warmth of the glowing red-hot stove until its dying embers gave way to the increasing cold. Then, stripped to underpants and vests, we sought warmth in our sheetless beds of straw and blankets. Throughout the night, we slept fitfully, beset by the two demons of cold and discomfort. The penetrating cold brought restlessness and groanings. From time to time ghost-like figures stumbled their way down the darkened aisle to relieve themselves in the bucket outside. Each time the door opened, chilled draughts of air swept down the hut. More than that, the blankets above and beneath us were rough and rasping so that, at every movement, they irritated our pampered skins. Neville, who was tall and skinny, suffered the most. I awakened to see that he had abandoned his bed to stand in the aisle, a shivering, stooping figure, enveloped in his blankets in an effort to keep warm.

If cold and discomfort were the demons that haunted our cossetted bodies, the winter of 1941 was the arch fiend. It became wickedly cold.

Heavy rains gave way to interminable frosts. The muddied ground became iron hard. In squad drills a shock wave travelled upwards through legs and spine to the brain with every stamping of the feet. Rigorous sessions of marching, physical training and weapon drill gave only temporary relief from the bitter cold. We craved for warmth. For a few hours at night, we sought it in the rays of the red-hot stove which we extravagantly fed with our limited ration of coke. All too soon, a rapidly cooling stove and the weariness of our tired, hard-worked bodies drove us quickly to our beds. Now, clothed in our army issue of winter vests and 'long john' pants and with our newly issued greatcoats serving as an extra blanket, the nights became more bearable and sleep more wholesome.

At the sound of Reveille we rose quickly, hustling and bustling with feverish haste. Beds were made up for inspection. There was constant movement, a dashing to and fro, to the ablutions hut. But amid this purposeful activity, a solitary figure, in an end bed, slept on, oblivious of sound and movement. The incumbent was 'Ginger', the hut corporal. He was lenient when judged by the exacting standards of the Training Centre. Early in the war, he had seen action in Norway with the Special Air Service and, it seemed, had returned from his experience a more tolerant soldier. He rarely chastised us and, after daily training was over, with regularity, he made up his corner bed and disappeared. Then, at some late hour, long after the sounding of the Last Post, he returned, often noisily, undressed in the dark and sank into deep repose.

Already, 'Ginger' had given strict orders not to be awakened until the breakfast bugle call. Then with indecent haste he sprang out of bed and dressed hurriedly, leaving his blankets in disarray. With bleary eyes he marched us to the dining hut.

There, we endured the daily fare of a Scottish Command porridge; a concoction generously laced with salt and having the consistency of clinging mud. How we hated the sugarless, salted, congealed mass and its concessionary helping of watered down evaporated milk. But our exacting training had brought on an insatiable appetite which overcame our distaste.

Ginger's benign regime bore no comparison with the iron discipline of 'Black Jock': a sergeant major of the Army Physical Training Corps, he filled us with awe and fear. He was awesome because of his past reputation. The news had spread that he had served for 32 years both in the Royal Navy and in the Army. More than that, he had been an All-India boxing champion. For an older man, he was exceptionally fit: his bony frame was lean and muscular; his nose was aquiline and he had the fearsome stare of an eagle, a stare made more sinister by one glass eye. In the hangar-like gymnasium we were always in nervous expectation of his coming. Even our younger Physical Training Instructors seemed in awe of him. A refusal to clear the vaulting horse would bring the threatening response, 'Don't let Black Jock hear you say you can't vault it.'

Whenever he appeared, striding purposefully along in his all-black track suit and wellington boots, our movements would become galvanized and we would clear the vaulting horse with alacrity.

Once, when our squad arrived at the hangar just two minutes late, Black Jock, with malevolent stare, awaited us. Ginger, who had marched us down, received the full force of his wrath and was ordered to move us, at the double, back to the Company Office. Black Jock followed and vented his anger on the orderlies. Meanwhile, outside, in vests and pants, our teeth chattering and our bodies frozen to the bones, we shivered in the penetrating cold. Eventually, Black Jock emerged and ordered Ginger to march us back to the comparative warmth of our unheated hut.

Another martinet was the Recruit Company's Training Officer. He had an overwhelming air of authority which engendered feelings of dislike in the ranks. During inspections, when he spoke with private soldiers, he had the irritating habit of beating the side of his leg with his stick of office. The more angry he became, the more he beat a tattoo on his leg. On one inspection, 'Bill', who was even shorter than I, had the effrontery to leave undone the top clasp on the collar of his battledress.

'Fasten that collar,' commanded the offended officer. 'What's your name?'

'Brassington,' was the innocent reply. This response raised the military hackles.

'Brassington, WHAT?' barked the officer.

'Brassington William,' Bill replied meekly.

There was a muffled hilarity in the ranks and on the face of the Training Officer a mixture of incredulity and disgust. This unwitting disrespect for the King's Commission was not Bill's only aberration. His inability to march in step with the rest of the squad was soon noticed. Because of his exceptionally short legs, he took more paces than was normal. This displeased not only our superiors but also the rest of Number Two Squad which was relegated to the shameful last place in the inter-squad marching competitions. Within days, our superiors acted. Bill left for service in the Pioneer Corps.

If inability to march was Bill's shortcoming, I remained conscious of my own disturbing traits. I was both sensitive and impetuous. From time to time, these traits surfaced to land me in trouble. At the outset of training, I had been taught to salute but with little idea of when not to salute. On one occasion, I was quickly reprimanded when I saluted an officer while half-dressed in gym shoes, vest and shorts. Worse was to follow when, along with another recruit, I was returning from 'piss' bucket duty. Suddenly, my comrade hissed out of the corner of his mouth, 'Salute, here's an officer on parade.'

In an instance of panic and in a moment of haste, I saluted smartly but entirely forgetful of the empty bucket dangling and clanking on my saluting arm. There was no escape from the wrath to come. An enraged captain thundered out the words, 'How long have you been in the Army?'

'Five days, Sir,' I replied fearfully.

The answer was my saving grace. There followed an upbraiding lecture explaining the rules of saluting. Fortunately, no charge of insulting behaviour was preferred.

A fortnight later, ill luck came. I was charged for being improperly dressed on my first fire picket inspection. A gas cape was my undoing. This piece of equipment was carried rolled up tightly on the shoulders above the small pack. It was fastened by string in a slip knot, with a length of the string hanging down the chest. When the string was pulled the knot would loosen and the cape would unroll, ready to be worn over the body. Unfortunately, just before the inspection of the guard, the gas cape unrolled involuntarily. I was aghast. The picket sergeant, noticing my dilemma, hastily rolled up the cape and tied a knot, a 'granny' it turned out to be rather than a slip knot. He was not a moment too soon. The Officer of the Guard had arrived – the thigh-tapping Training Officer. Down the ranks he marched with a tall, ginger-haired sergeant-major in tow. Occasionally, he stopped to inspect a recruit.

Inevitably, he stopped before me. I was closely examined as the stick moved against his thigh like a metronome. Then misfortune struck. He pulled the gas cape string. The cape remained in place. Again, a harder tug. The cape refused to drop. Turning to the Warrant Officer, he spoke the fateful words,

'Sergeant-Major Murphy, put this man on a charge!'

On the next morning, to answer the charge, I appeared on company orders, was found guilty of being improperly dressed, and was sentenced to two days of extra duties.

In reality, the two days of extra duties became two evenings of pack drill. I was ordered to wear field service marching order. Ginger, the hut corporal came to my rescue and found time before his evening's foray to show me how to wear the 'impedimenta' I had piled on my bed.

On a framework of webbing belt and shoulder straps, he hung a heavy, large pack; to the belt he fastened a small pack, Bren gun ammunition pouches, water bottle, bayonet and scabbard. Above the pouches, he fastened to my chest a gas mask in a canvas container. The offending gas cape was positioned on the shoulders above the large pack. In addition, I wore a steel helmet and carried a short Lee-Enfield rifle.

Loaded like a pack mule and feeling like one, I set off for the parade ground where I found two other heavily burdened defaulters awaiting the arrival of the Regimental Police sergeant.

For twenty minutes, he marched or doubled us to and fro. Before long, the perspiration formed, gathered and rolled down our reddened faces. From our sweating bodies, it seeped through our battledress and, where the webbing touched it, it darkened the coating of blanco so laboriously applied each day. Our ordeal came to an end unmercifully, for, in the remaining minutes, we were ordered to double to and fro, while we were wearing our gas masks.

Twice, then, we endured the body-racking punishment and we returned to our quarters breathless, nauseated and exhausted. On throwing off our burdens, with dismay, we noticed that our webbing equipment was marked heavily with the sweat stains of our exertions. There followed the added impositions of nightly scrubbings with bleached water and the constant new applications of blanco before the webbing became so acceptably clean that it would pass the frequent inspections.

Basic training went on apace. 'Square bashing' continued unabated until we responded automatically to marching commands. Soon, it gave place to practice with weapons other than rifles. Our attention was given to that most versatile of infantry weapons, the Bren light machine-gun. Theoretically, we learned that it was, 'capable of a high and rapid rate of fire with the employment of few men.' Even in our practice, there were overtones of the drill time of 'one, two, three, one'. In the naming of the parts we chanted 'clips-bi-pod-bren'. But it was in the dismantling and re-assembling of the gun that we took most pleasure and soon became experts.

The two-inch mortar, we were told, fired bombs with a high trajectory and a steep angle of descent and was capable of laying a smokescreen rapidly. We handled unprimed Number 36 Mills hand grenades, apprehensive of the time when we would throw our first primed one.

On the range at Dumfries, we fired live ammunition. It was then that we felt the recoil of a rifle and the thump it gave to the shoulder; the judder of the Bren gun as we struggled to control the short bursts of fire. In camp, we entered the gas chamber not only to check the efficiency of our gas masks but also to remove them; to experience both streaming eyes and the smell of pear drops associated with the gas.

As training progressed so six weeks were completed. The transformation from civilian to soldier was quickening. We changed our quarters when the Recruit Company was broken up. Some who could drive vehicles joined the Armoured Car Company. The rest were subjected to a non-verbal reasoning test (a verbal reasoning test would have suited me better). In the test I must have fared badly for those who had done well were drafted to a Driver Mechanics Company. But what of the remainder of which I was one? We were posted to Number 4 Company to be trained as Assault Troops.

At the other side of the camp we found our accommodation; another plain Nissen hut like the last, but, between its two corrugated iron skins, like poltergeists, there roamed rats and mice. Throughout the night they scampered to and fro, their feet beating a tattoo on the corrugations. With bravado, they ventured into our living space, much to the chagrin of 'Dick', who slept alongside me. He received nightly visits by mice which seemed to be attracted by some edible content of his hair cream. They sucked his hair.

It was in Number 4 Company that one of our number cracked. 'Froggy', deciding that he had had enough, took to his bed, refused to rise and went without food. Furthermore, in the words of his charge sheet, he 'passed faeces', soiling his blankets and underclothing. The Regimental Police came, lifted him - bed, blankets and all - carried him down to the River Annan and dumped him into the icy water. Having been forced to rinse his blankets and scrub himself clean, he was taken to the Detention Hut. We did not see him again.

For us who soldiered on, the winter's cold intensified. The coming of heavy snows curtailed our training. But there was no relief from toil. For two days we laboured to clear the snowdrifts from the A74, the main road to Glasgow. Without the help of today's snow ploughs, armed only with shovels and working like navvies, we dug from drift to drift, from daylight to dusk until, wearily, we scrambled into trucks cheered by the thoughts of a hot meal and the luxury of a night's sleep.

Another diversion from routine came when we spent a day's hunting with the Halleaths pack of beagles. We set off in denims and army boots and soon we were charging across the bone-hard, furrowed fields, only the lying snow cushioning our tread. We followed the chasing hounds with glee, rejoicing in our temporary freedom. At the end of the hunt, with our cheeks glowing and our bodies pleasantly warmed, we returned in the late afternoon, disappointed only that the hounds had not started a single hare.

On one evening, we were reminded of the tragedy that war brings. At short notice, several of us were hastily formed into a section to mount a 24-hour guard on the wreckage of a Hurricane fighter plane. The aircraft, on a flight from Crosby-on-Eden air station, had flown at high speed into a hillside, disintegrating and burying its engine deep into the ground. In the wreckage, we found a bent and distorted chrome identity disc bearing the words, 'Flying Officer W Andrew Campbell, Ontario, Canada'.

At night, we carried out our lonely, funereal vigil. By day, we deterred a constant trail of sightseers and souvenir hunters, who wound their way upwards by an ever-darkening pathway through the lying snow.

Having done its worst, the snow retreated. Winter gave way to spring. In camp, our basic training was ending. In anticipation we looked forward to the passing-out parade, spurred on by the news that the parade was to be conducted by none other than that doyen of warrant officers, Regimental Sergeant-Major Brittain of the Brigade of Guards. We began a frenetic 'bulling-up' of all our equipment. Hours were spent in the polishing and boning of our boots until the toe caps were as smooth and shining as black marble; our brasses were polished until they threatened to outdo the sun; and the inside creases of our battledress trousers were so carefully soaped and pressed between our mattresses and bed boards that the outside creases became as sharp as butchers' knives.

When the great day came, we responded nobly to the Regimental Sergeant-Major's august and commanding presence and to his precise and trenchant orders. After his inspection, with a feeling of relief and expectation we were dismissed. Now our basic training was at an end. Within days, along with a few of my friends, I left for a short stay in the 48th Reconnaissance Company.

Two

One Step Nearer to Battle

In a draft of twenty men, we left the Halleaths Training Centre for Lincolnshire. The 48th Independent Reconnaissance Company was encamped in the grounds of a country house near to the village of Baumber. Its soldiers were almost entirely Scotsmen, having served previously in a disbanded Territorial battalion of the Highland Light Infantry. Older men than we were, they turned out to be ardently clannish. They spoke with a Glaswegian accent and with such machine-gun rapidity that we struggled to follow their lingo. For headgear they wore Balmorals which in contrast with our less glamorous side caps made our small English contingent look conspicuously different.

Most of the Scotsmen came from Glasgow. Some, it seemed, were Gorbals toughened. In their barrack-room talk, such names as Barlinnie Gaol and its colloquial description 'the glass house' were often heard, leaving us Sassenachs to believe that some might have been inside the place. Christian names such as Jimmy and Danny were common among them, suggesting a Scots-Irish descent.

They played soccer with passion and enthusiasm. When our small group of Sassenachs took them on, we were beaten time and again. But their enthusiasm for 'footba' was not matched by their zeal in training. Having been in the Territorial Army before and since the war began, their interest had waned as their full-time service lengthened. Lack of interest manifested itself when the platoon began bayonet practice. Some of them were unimpressed by the rhetoric when told that, 'The object of bayonet fighting was that a man should have confidence in his own and his comrade's skill with the weapon, thereby imbued with grim

14

determination to close with the enemy.'

After such theory came the practice. Bayonet training took place in the camp woodlands, where a number of strong, wooden frames, on which straw filled sandbags had been stretched, awaited our attacks. Fresh from the Training Centre, we young Sassenachs dashed from frame to frame, yelling enthusiastically, 'In! Out! On guard!' as we thrust our bayonets into the inanimate straw filled hessian. In contrast, Danny and Spud, the old hands, used their bayonets lethargically, silently exhibiting a kind of dumb insolence, a protest against the savagery of the practice and the 'system' they had come to abhor.

Beating the 'system' remained their preoccupation. Danny, a physically powerful, strong-willed man, had the aura of a gang leader. Others, including 'Spud', seemed to be influenced and manipulated by him. Danny's forte was stealing. On one evening, when the company paraded for a talk about Lawrence of Arabia by Sir Ronald Storrs, Danny and 'Spud' furtively absented themselves. On our return to the hut, we found the two absentees consuming bacon 'butties' rifled from a deserted cookhouse.

Danny's aberrations were not confined to camp. As a truck driver, opportunities arose to pursue his devious ways. Once, during an army exercise, when the 48th Company acted as the enemy, he contrived to have his truck 'knocked out' by adjudicating officers. No longer in battle, he absconded for two days, driving home to Glasgow and back again before the exercise ended.

Retribution came on a second army scheme in Lincolnshire. From a convenient military petrol dump, by deceit, he stole petrol which he sold to civilian black marketeers. He was caught in the act, taken into custody, convicted and was seen no more.

Another Danny, of a different mould, was conspicuous by his eccentricity. His great obsession was to get out of the Army by being certified mentally unsound. Constantly, he plagued the Orderly Room staff by pinning to the door a crudely painted poster bearing the inscription '1950 will come!' This same message was permanently knitted into his army pullover both in front and at the back. Often, in a raucous voice, he could be heard portending the coming of 1950. His superiors were not impressed, turning a blind eye to his demonstrations. Sadly, for Danny, 1950 never came. He was killed by shell fire in the Anzio Beach Head.

It was during my stay in the 48th that I had two confrontations with authority. Both were concerned with my appearance. Throughout my early training, in the face of numerous inspections by hawk-eyed instructors, I had avoided the imposition of shaving. I was fresh of face with hardly discernable wispy, facial hair. But my deception ended on a sunny morning when the company paraded for inspection. The early morning sun shone almost horizontally down the ranks, its rays highlighting the blonde hairs on my chin. Along the ranks strode an irate sergeant-major. He stopped to face me. Then with leering eyes and with rasping voice, he uttered the censorious words, 'Get that bum fluff off!'

My razor-free days were over. I was twenty years old, and the delayed manifestation of my manhood had come to stay.

A second encounter with authority occurred when I came face to face with the Company Police Sergeant. He was a dour, heavily built man, who, rather than walk smartly along the camp pathways, skulked and crept about in a stealthy manner. He appeared when least expected, walking with a bowed head as if searching the ground. But most mystifying was his peculiar mannerism of agitating his right fist like a gambler shaking dice. I was to discover the secret when he confronted me with the remark, 'A button missing lad. Improperly dressed. Why?'

Unfortunately, there was a button missing from my denim overalls. I made the lame excuse of having used up all the buttons in my 'housewife' hold-all. Triumphantly, he opened his huge fist to reveal a variety of buttons collected in his perambulations. I was hoping vainly that he would offer me one of these but, he growled sardonically, 'What are these, lad? Scotch bl—dy mist?'

It was in the 48th that the role of a reconnaissance company (soon to be called a squadron) became clearer. A squadron was divided into three scout troops, one assault troop and squadron headquarters. The scout troops were equipped with lightly armoured cars called Beaverettes and tracked vehicles called Bren carriers. The assault troop, of four sections of riflemen, was carried in 15cwt trucks. In simple terms, the tactics were that the armoured cars went forward to seek and contact the enemy. On contact, the Bren carriers would dash forward to consolidate on the land gained, the assault troop being ready to attack stubborn, enemy defences.

For the assault troop, tactics apart, there was specialized training in the use of explosives. With this in mind, several of us were sent on an Explosives Course. In two sections, each riding in a 15cwt truck, we set off for a camp at Woodhall Spa. Unpleasant surprises awaited us. Danny, an expert in driving, set a fast rate. Neville, the driver of our truck, having just passed his driving test, endeavoured to keep pace but, on a left hand bend, he lost control. Fearfully, we huddled in the back, helplessly awaiting the outcome, powerless to do anything. The truck zigzagged from side to side of the road until it ran up a grassy bank, turning over on its side and spilling us out like sacks of potatoes. Momentarily I was stunned, but recovered to realize that my spectacles had disappeared. Some minutes later I found them unbroken, several yards away. My injuries were not serious. I had a rapidly closing eye, cuts on my hands and face and two bumps on my head even though I wore a steel helmet. The effect of the impact had caused the half mess tin in my greatcoat pocket to bend almost double and tear through the khaki cloth.

Of the others in the truck, some were taken to hospital. Some, including myself, cleaned ourselves up at a wayside house and elected to carry on with the course. A relief truck came to take us to our destination. On arrival, we little thought that another frightening experience was in the offing. In the afternoon, we started the explosive course in one of the ubiquitous Nissen huts. It was empty except for two or three rows of forms, a blackboard and easel and an army mess table. Against the sides of the hut had been piled explosives such as gun cotton and primers, detonators and the high explosive, amanol.

A Sergeant Instructor arrived and we sat down to watch his demonstration of the making of booby traps using a battery, two lengths of wire and a tiny pile of gunpowder which he took from a metal box on the table; the gunpowder being ignited when the two ends of wire were put into the pile. He repeated the experiment twice, each time causing the gunpowder to flare rather than explode. For a third time, the gunpowder flared but so did the gunpowder in the box. From a round hole in the lid of the box, there came a column of flame followed by an unexpected explosion, the force of which blew us backwards over our forms. We struggled to our feet in dense smoke, groping our way towards the door, emerging with blackened faces and our eyebrows and greatcoats singed. Later, as we recovered from the ordeal, we were horrified to learn that the explosives along the walls could have been set off by a phenomenon known as 'sympathetic detonation'.

Still alive, battered and weary by the day's happenings, we sought our beds and restorative powers of sleep. For a while, we were denied even this luxury. Close to the perimeter of the army camp was a Royal Air Force Bomber Command Station with its complement of the first operational Lancaster bombers, their runway approaching to within yards of our sleeping quarters. At intervals, they 'taxied' towards us, turned and with their four engines under full eardrum bursting power, thrust into the night, bound for Germany. Eventually, our tired bodies were not to be denied and we sank into a deep sleep.

On the following morning, refreshed and resilient in our youthfulness, we resumed training. For the remainder of the course, we explored the potential of explosives. With necklaces of gelignite and gun cotton primers, we destroyed aged and decaying trees; with Bangalore torpedoes (metal piping packed with explosive) we blew gaps in barbed wire entanglements and, without realizing their destructive power, we were taught to prime the Mark Four anti-tank mine and the Number 75 anti-personnel mine.

On completion of the course, we returned to camp and its routine of training and duties. There, life was pleasantly tolerable and far from demanding. The fine weather of early summer suited us and we flourished in good health and in feelings of well being. For the most part, the weekends were long and free. They began after the regular Saturday morning cleaning of the barrack-room. The chore of sweeping and cleaning was given the high-sounding euphemism of 'interior economy'. We swept and tidied with great gusto, knowing that after inspection we were free. Then, like schoolboys after school was over, we dashed away to the pleasures of Lincoln or other nearby towns.

Suddenly, after four idyllic weeks, our stay in the 48th came to an abrupt end. With great haste, a group of mostly Englishmen was ordered to attend for an overseas medical examination. As we left the barrack-room. 'Spud' gave us his advice. Couched in his usual contemptible manner, he suggested that we ought to swallow a small piece of soap to contrive rapid heartbeats in order to fail the medical examination. None heeded his counsel and each of us was passed fit for overseas service.

The rapidity at which we were posted surprised us. By the following day, without ceremony or farewells, in field service marching order carrying full kitbags we set off to join the 1st Reconnaissance Regiment of the 1st British Infantry Division. Our journey by train and truck ended in the heathlands, near Thetford, Norfolk.

Three

A Further Step to Battle

R iddlesworth Camp lay astride the Garboldisham Road. Half
hidden by brush and trees were wooden huts and armoured
vehicles. The quietness and peace of the woodlands was being
disturbed by cars' engines, men's voices and marching feet; feet
that marched at Light Infantry pace or even doubled from place
to place. Urgency and purpose seemed to permeate through the
camp. I was surprised to observe a lone officer, practising with
serious intent by drawing, aiming and replacing his revolver in
the accepted Wild West manner. That the regiment was bracing
itself for battle seemed without doubt.

With no delay, six of us were paraded before the commander of
'C' Squadron, 'Major R R'. In demeanour, he exuded confidence
and efficiency. In appearance, he was cast in the 'Montgomery'
mould. He had Monty's same sharp, almost fox-like features, the
same clipped, military moustache and the same pointed, determined
speech.

On his inspection, I reported that I had been trained as an
assault trooper. His face showed that he was not impressed by my
physical attributes. A quick scrutiny of my physique brought a
correspondingly quick response in words which were destined to
alter the whole course of my life in the regiment. He said,
'Sergeant-Major! This man to 16 Troop, gunner light armoured
car or Bren carrier. Put him down for a wireless course.' With
these words, I was initiated into the ranks of 16 Troop.

Sixteen Troop was a fusion of regular soldiers with battle
experience and conscripts of inexperience who were younger men.
The older 'regulars' could tell of long service in India. Formerly,
they were infantrymen of the 3rd Infantry Brigade of 1st British

Infantry Division. In their new role, they found it hard to forget their old regimental pride and ties. In a way, they still considered themselves to be either 'Dukes' (lst Battalion, the Duke of Wellington's Regiment) or 'Foresters' (2nd Battalion, the Nottinghamshire and Derby Regiment) or 'Kislis' (1st Battalion, the King's Shropshire Light Infantry). Their speech was adorned with Hindustani words. Beds were always *charpoys* and rifles *bondouks*. Tea was always *char* and the 'Deolali Tap' was equated not only with sunstroke but also with eccentricity or mental abnormality. On the outbreak of war, they went to France with the British Expeditionary Force. After the 'phoney war', they fought in the rearguard action before being evacuated from the beaches of Dunkirk. Their experience had placed most of them in positions of authority. In a generous ratio of one to every two troopers, they were our non-commissioned officers.

As conscripts, we troopers had no such bonding or experience. We came from the length and breadth of Britain. Topography was the starting point for the friendship groups which emerged. Five or six Geordies became very closely acquainted so much so that throughout the ensuing campaigns they shared bivouacs and dug-outs. There was a small group of Yorkshiremen who had been conscripted and trained in their home county. From the south of the Watford Gap came several men but the oddest friendship group of all was the 'Bicycle Club' of which I was one of three whose only common factor was the wearing of spectacles, an uncommon occurrence in a front line formation.

Our billets were wooden huts devoid of chairs and bedside cupboards. Our beds served for both sleep and relaxation as well as for the laying out of kit for frequent inspection. George, the hut corporal, exercised a strict control within the hut. He was serious and remote, disapproving of our inadequacies often with irony and derision. We were judged by the letter of the law rather than by its spirit. Every morning, he was up and dressed before the call of Reveille. Almost before the last notes had died away, he was moving along the aisle, snatching blankets from the recumbent bodies of those who did not rise immediately. Even on Sunday evenings we were not free of his impositions. 'Tich', the only one with a portable radio, provided us with a musical treat. In the late evening, we luxuriated on our beds, listening to the soothing, syrupy voice of Ann Shelton in her programme, *Introducing Ann.* Our enjoyment was cut short at the sounding of the Last Post; 'Tich' was ordered to switch off the dulcet sounds, out would go the lights and talking had to cease.

In the exercise of discipline, George was unrelenting but little were we to know that, hidden behind the screen of regimentation, was a brave and kindly heart which, in the heat of battle, manifested itself in distinguished conduct. The discipline we met in Corporal George had its origins in the influence and actions of the regimental commander. He, in turn, while serving in Southern Command had been influenced by none other than General Montgomery, its commander.

In preparing the regiment for battle, the regimental commander insisted that the individual's physical fitness was of paramount importance. From Southern Command, he brought Monty's concept of 'Binge', an early morning daily discipline for all ranks including himself. It was on Binge that he was most conspicuous. Shortly after Reveille, in a brilliant yellow sweater, he made his appearance. His apparel and his habit of flitting in and out of the huts and through the woodlands, prompted us to nickname him 'The Canary'. As he pursued his lonely Binge we too were on the move, doubling through the camp dressed in vest, braced trousers, stockings and army boots. After thirty minutes, the imposition was over and we returned with the blood coursing through our veins and an heightened hunger for breakfast.

Each Friday afternoon came a seven-mile cross-country run. Again, only soldiers on duties were excused. Always, at the start and prominent in yellow sweater, 'The Canary' appeared. As a gesture, he ran for the first mile with us and then eased his aging body into his convenient staff car for the short journey back to await our return.

'The Canary' was a firm believer in exhortation and homily. His regimental orders began with one or the other. Most were concerned with physical fitness. Others reminded us of the importance of keeping our armoured vehicles in tip-top condition. One such exhortation read, 'Maintenance in the battlefield is second only to battle.'

A great deal of our working day was spent on looking after our vehicles. Hours were long and there were six working days in each week, Sunday being just another working day. We developed a close relationship with our armoured cars and Bren carriers. We became familiar with every part right down to the smallest split pin. Our relationship was so close that we began to personify our vehicles with such words as, 'Go and get her filled up,' or of her engine, 'She'll have to have an oil change today.'

Like the cavalry horses our vehicles had replaced, after tactical training they came first and were refuelled and checked before we could stand down. More than that, we tended and groomed them with oily rags dipped in petrol, laced with SAE 30 engine oil, to give their outward appearance a sheen which would not disgrace a well-groomed charger.

It was in these days of preparation for battle that an unknown lyricist composed a morale boosting verse to the tune of *Anchors Aweigh*. It read:

> 'Carriers away, my lads, carriers away,
> You're the spearhead of Division,
> Bags of "Binge" and quick decision.
> Carriers in gear, my lads,
> Humberettes "revved up",
> Fingers on the Bren gun triggers,
> In you go, my lads, the best of luck.'

Tactical training went on apace. We began to practise some of the roles expected of us. On several occasions, both by night and by day, the bridge at Brettenham became the object of a 'seize and hold' role. We practised 'making contact' with the 'enemy' (on one occasion Home Guards from Thetford). A new word, 'laager', entered our vocabulary and soon we became familiar with the drill of making a defensive encampment with a circle of vehicles. When travelling in convoy, with practised skill, at every stop, to the cry of 'nets on', we disguised each vehicle in camouflaged netting. At the end of the stoppage, from the front of the convoy, came the order, 'Nets off! Start up!' and we would be on the move again.

Apart from our schemes outside of the camp, freedom to leave was restricted to one day in each week. On the day appointed, each of the squadrons, in turn, ceased all duties for exactly 24 hours, from midnight to midnight of the next day. Anyone arriving back beyond the bounds of that time was immediately charged with being absent without leave and was duly punished.

Within the camp, freedom and relaxation from the long hours of work was confined to a morning and afternoon break for tea in the NAAFI canteen. It was of no wonder that all other ranks became highly incensed when orders were given that our tea breaks would cease. The pretext was that the war in Burma had been lost in the NAAFI canteens of India and that drinking tea had contributed towards the retreat to the Indian border. With this cruel imposition work rate declined and resentment grew. Its repercussions were felt first in the orderly rooms and, subsequently, in the ranks of our superiors. Within two days, the order was rescinded and we joyfully drank the notorious NAAFI tea again.

As summer gave way to autumn and the falling leaves, training at Riddlesworth Camp came to an end. The regiment was at full strength and virtually ready for action. As for myself, Major RR's plan to make me into a wireless operator was about to reach fruition. After a preliminary course in camp, I went to finish my training in a Royal Signals training depot at the Karrier Works in Huddersfield. At the end of my course in both radio telephony and wireless telegraphy I was given leave. On my return to camp, I was surprised and mystified not only by its deserted look but also by its lack of the usual hustle and bustle. Of the Regiment's armour there was no sign. Forlorn, I wandered around until I came across a rear party of one or two men under the command of the regiment's anti-tank troop sergeant. From him I received the news that, in my absence, the regiment had moved to Rothesay, on the Isle of Bute. There, for a fortnight, its squadrons were to be trained in the loading and off-loading of vehicles in and out of LSTs (Tank Landing Ships). Meanwhile, along with the rear party, I was to travel by train to the seaside village of West Kilbride, on the Ayrshire coast. There I was to help prepare Crosby House, one of the homes of the Duke of Hamilton which had been requisitioned for the use of C Squadron.

On arrival at the mansion, I was paired with another conscript of 16 Troop, 'Cockney George'. Our task was to make ready the house. We found the rooms bare of furniture and carpets. The floors and fireplaces awaited our cleaning operations. By the time

C Squadron had arrived the house was ready for occupation. The men of 16 Troop were allotted an upstairs room which was grossly overcrowded. Each man's groundsheet and blankets were separated only from the next man's by his kitbag and equipment. This overcrowding brought incidences of scabies, the old soldiers called them 'crabs'. More than that, a few men, following liaisons with loose women, had contracted venereal disease. On a visit to the squadron, The Canary was furious at this lowering of morals and went so far as to say that the fighting efficiency of the regiment was already being impaired. But his real purpose in addressing us was to bring the sobering news that in about two weeks' time the regiment would be in action, softening his momentous words by assuring us that there would be no unnecessary loss of life while under his command.

So we settled down to wait. The northern days were short with lowering skies. The nights were long and dreary. Night guard duties, the private soldier's bane, came round frequently. In between the two-hourly stretches of duty, somewhat wearily, we rested fully dressed. We lay about a coal fire, uncomfortable in our equipment. In the light of the fire, we stared at the carved lettering on the oak mantelpiece above. The words, ironic under the circumstances, exhorted us to:

'Be noble, and the nobleness that lies in other men, sleeping, but never dead, will rise in majesty to meet thine own.'

In off-duty hours, there was little to do. Occasionally, we were allowed to hitch-hike to Glasgow or Paisley, but the most resourceful soldier was 'Johnny', the second in command of the Squadron. He elected to send for his fishing tackle and spent his leisure hours fly-fishing in a nearby burn.

Suddenly, we lost our armour. In Ardrossan, it was loaded into ships of a convoy bound for where we, in the ranks, did not know. We were left only with our weapons. Because our departure was imminent, we were fed for the first time from field kitchens. Simple, unvaried food was contrived. With monotonous regularity there was boiled rice for sweet. Daily it dropped heavily into our waiting mess tins, a glutinous mass. As usual Cockney George responded with a witticism:

'They must think we're bl—dy Chinks.'

The perpetrator of our unenterprising meals was not the chief cook, Corporal Bill, but his superior, Quartermaster Sergeant Bill. Previously, one of our number overheard the following exchange of words between the two,

Corporal Cook Bill: 'What about a jam roly-poly for the lads, for a change?'

Quartermaster Sergeant Bill: (without much deliberation, and in a disparaging way) 'F—k 'em! Give 'em rice!'

So it was rice we had to endure until our time at last ran out.

One evening, we in the ranks heard the news that, early on the following morning, we would be leaving for an unknown destination. Before light, at five on the morning, 28 February 1943, dressed in full equipment and carrying our weapons we marched to West Kilbride station. Our departure, supposedly, was a secret but it seemed that the whole of the village population had come to see us off. We boarded the train and, having been issued with haversack rations, a long journey was anticipated. So, with aplomb, we removed our boots and settled comfortably in our seats, while, at the open windows, the more worldly wise soldiers, having developed esoteric relationships with lonely women, said their last goodbyes.

Eventually, we steamed away. A half-hour later, our predictions of a long journey were hopelessly wrong for the train entered the King George V Dock in the port of Glasgow. As we detrained at the quayside, we saw, lying low in the water and looking smaller than her 14,000 tons, the troopship the *Dunottar Castle*.

On board, we descended gangway by gangway into the bowels of the ship until we reached a lower deck close to the waterline. Our quarters were lit only by artificial light, the portholes being closed. A feeling of claustrophobia was heightened by a low ceiling, made lower by rows of racks and by lines of hooks for the slinging of hammocks. Below, at floor level, stood long rows of anchored mess tables and forms, which, at meal times, were crowded with men. At night, they became repositories for untidy piles of shed clothing. At one end of the deck, huge box-like storage cupboards reduced the living space. By night they were empty, by day they were filled with stowed hammocks.

Thankfully, our weapons had been deposited in the ship's armoury and we had dispensed with our boots in favour of plimsolls. Each of us was given a bulky, kapok-filled lifebelt which rested uncomfortably on our shoulders and gripped our chests like a strait-jacket, but, owing to our perilous sea journey, these had to be worn frequently. At night, they made acceptable hammock pillows.

We sailed at noon, steaming down the Clyde. On either bank, the ship and tank builders, in their dinner break, waved us by. We responded cheerfully, our high spirits belying more sober thoughts of how long it would be before our return or whether we would return at all.

In the Firth of Clyde, the convoy grew. It was joined by its escorts of a destroyer and two frigates as it sailed southwards through the Irish Sea and into Atlantic waters. Aboard, we began to settle into a routine. We were told of our destination, the port of Algiers. Pamphlets were issued to all which contained a code of conduct for troops on active service in North Africa. In them we were told not to spit near a mosque, not to ridicule grown Arab men who walked hand in hand and, above all, not to ogle or liaise with Arab women.

By word of mouth, we were told that we would be joining General Anderson's First Army with its axis of advance centred on the Medjerda valley and the small town of Medjez El Bab, in Tunisia.

On board, we followed a daily routine which hardly varied. At daybreak we rose, freeing ourselves from the embracing folds of our hammocks. Cat like, we dropped on to the mess tables and dressed. At our ablutions we rinsed in the obligatory salt water, our soaps lying uselessly in our small packs for we could not raise a lather. Shaving was cruel torment and we were glad to return to our living space. There, hammocks were unslung, rolled and stowed away. Breakfast followed with its additional odours and warmth to add to the fetid atmosphere compounded by two hundred perspiring bodies and a million or more night-time respirations. Always we were glad to ascend the gangways and to savour the fresh sea breezes of the upper deck.

On and below decks, there were duties to perform. Some of us were assigned to swabbing the wooden deck; others to mess duties below. There were frequent lifeboat and raft drills but, usually, afternoons were free and, as we steamed ever further southwards in increasing heat and sunshine, we lounged and idled the hours away.

Beyond us, over the water, the frigates and destroyer maintained their protective screen while the ships of the convoy kept station, sailing line astern in three rows. On one afternoon, we were surprised when the *Dunottar Castle* dropped astern. As the convoy receded, so the gunners of the Maritime Regiment began preparing their stern mounted twelve-pounder gun for firing practice. As they worked, a small brown bird, miles from the nearest land, landed on the turntable platform only to be killed instantly by the blast of the first shot. The incident renewed my sensitivity to hurt and came as a reminder that, in warfare, death was always close at hand.

The firing practice over, the ship raised speed and quickly caught up with the slower moving convoy. At an average of 300 nautical miles in each 24 hours, the ships sailed on. There had been no enemy interference either by air or by sea until, towards the end of the voyage, the convoy sailed off course for a whole day in order to avoid an enemy submarine pack.

Against the dawn, on the ninth day, the North African coast appeared darkly, and later came a blaze of shore lights marking the neutral city of Tangier. As the sun rose, out of the dark sea loomed the imposing outline of the Rock of Gibraltar while beneath its towering shoulder, in the daylight, the harbour below and the nearby Spanish coastal towns gleamed white in the morning sunshine.

We anchored in the Straits where the Atlantic flotilla of escort ships left us, while, from out of the harbour, the Mediterranean flotilla appeared to take up the task of protecting us on the final sail to Algiers. Soon, we weighed anchor and sailed eastwards under blue skies and in calm waters. Behind us, a shoal of porpoises kept pace, leaping and cavorting in the wake. Less numerous flying fish skimmed over the water, their blue fins beating the alien air.

By night, to avoid the stifling heat below, most of us remained on deck until a late hour. On the after deck, leaning on the guard rails, we watched the phosphorous glowing in the foaming wake.

Above, the star-studded sky reminded us that under that self-same sky now, not a great distance away, the First and Eighth Armies were locked in battle with the German Afrika Korps.

In the late afternoon of the tenth day at sea, the city of Algiers came into view. As we passed by the entrance to the harbour, we were greeted with the jeers of the crew of a Bofors anti-aircraft gun.

'You're too late, the war's over,' was their message. Little did they know that the next six weeks of vicious warfare would have proved them ignorantly wrong.

No sooner had the *Donottar Castle* berthed than we were in the midst of an air raid. Enemy intelligence was aware of our time of arrival. From down below, we heard the 'crumps' of bombs and the continuous 'thumps' of anti-aircraft gunfire. Hurriedly, a piper of the Sixth Gordon Highlanders was summoned to play Scottish airs as we waited to disembark.

After the raid, having spent ten days at sea, we pushed our cosseted feet into army boots again, collected our weapons, donned our equipment and prepared for a long night march to a transit camp some twelve miles away. We began the 'foot-slog' marching by troops in threes. Before long we were in disarray, disintegrating into unregimented, disparate groups of men, spreading over long stretches of road.

In C Squadron, only the riflemen of the assault troop were able to maintain a steady and orderly pace. We, in the scout troops, were burdened with our heavier weapons, the encumbering Boyes anti-tank rifles, our eight Bren guns and a pair of two-inch mortars. To speed our progress we initiated a plan. Each anti-tank rifle would be carried by two men; Bren guns and two-inch mortars would be partly dismantled and shared. Even then, we could not keep pace with the riflemen who carried their weapons comfortably slung on their shoulders. They drew further ahead as the night wore on.

Every ten minutes in the hour, we paused for rest, some to fall asleep until, at the end of the break, they were roughly shaken into action by our sergeants. In the last pause before dawn broke, Cockney George wearily sank down beside a resting soldier and asked him to sit back to back for a little comfort and warmth. To Cockney George's surprise he found that it was 'The Canary' who had marched all the way alongside his men. But such was the disorder that, having reached the transit camp and having been issued with blankets and sent to sleep in a large marquee, I awoke to find that I had been sleeping between the Squadron Sergeant-Major and the Quartermaster Sergeant.

Discouraging news came to the transit camp. Eighteen of our armoured cars were lost at sea owing to an enemy attack on the vehicles' convoy. From Regimental Headquarters, the news filtered through that some of us might have to reconnoitre in Jeeps, a daunting prospect when we realized their vulnerability to even small arms fire.

Quickly, we were reunited with our remaining armour and ordered to move to the docks in Algiers. Once there, along with the Bren carriers of the 24th Guards Brigade, we boarded two awaiting LSTs bound for the small port of Bone, close to the Tunisian border.

The two LSTs became part of a small convoy of ships, some oilers and coasters of much smaller tonnage. We set sail in the evening, hugging the coastline. That we were drawing closer to the battle zone became evident. Around the upper deck of our ship, at intervals, we manned Bren guns mounted on tripods, in readiness to respond to any enemy air attacks. Throughout the night, we slept fully dressed on tiered bunks as, under cover of darkness, without lights, the convoy sailed steadily onwards.

At five o'clock in the morning, the ship's strident alarm sounded. We were loath to leave our bunks until an anxious sergeant appeared and ordered us to rush to our lifeboat station. In the darkness, on the upper deck, we remained on our station, seeing little and hearing nothing but the ship's engine and the lapping of the sea. When dawn broke, in the light of day, we were ordered to stand down. From a sailor who had been on night duty, we were given an account of the raid by enemy submarines. Two had been lying in wait in inlets of the coast rather than out at sea. Simultaneously, they had launched torpedo attacks on the two larger LSTs. In each case, four torpedoes had been fired. Three had made fluorescent trails as they sped across the bows and one had passed directly underneath our LST, amidships. According to the sailor, we were saved from disaster by the shallow draft of the landing craft.

By noon, without interference, we docked in the harbour at Bone, off-loading our armour and travelling inland to 'laager' for the night, close to some swampy ground. There, throughout the night, legions of frogs croaked in continuous chorus disturbing our sleeping hours.

Transportation by sea was now over. For the remaining stage of our journey to the front line we would move forward by road. Soon 16 Troop's soldiers would be seeing action. But, who were these men and what of their armour?

'Davy' was our troop commander. In physique, he was short and stiff. He rarely smiled and spoke sparingly. His countenance was that of serious man, more aware, perhaps, that his was the ultimate responsibility for the troop's actions in battle.

Davy's chief subordinate, at this time, was 'John Bill', his troop sergeant. A Yorkshireman, he had been a regular soldier for a long time. Unlike the loud voiced, conventional sergeant, he was more of a father figure. In his muted voice, one could detect a sense of humour, no bad trait when life was tough. One physical trait marked him out; his shuffling gait and a disposition to be turkey-toed as he walked.

The two carrier section sergeants were 'Tac', a Welshman, and Tex. Both were regulars. Of the two, Tac was the more stable and predictable. On the other hand, Tex was the maverick. Of average height and wiry, he had strikingly blonde hair with a close clipped moustache to match. There were two sides to his nature. On the one hand, he was smart, convincing and flamboyant, but on the other, he was audacious, impulsive and unpredictable. Often he flouted army conventions. His past army life had been marked with a propensity to rise and fall in rank at a whim, fluctuating in rank between that of sergeant and private soldier. He was soon to follow his inclinations again.

In his Bren carrier crew were 'Dinky', his driver, and myself, his Bren gunner, christened 'Young Niss' by Cockney George. Some insight into my traits are already known: of Dinky none until now. He was born and bred in Birchgrove, a suburb of Cardiff. Before conscription, he worked for Hans Renold Chains and was to display in battle the steely strength of the chains he produced. Always unruffled, he was fortified by the experience of driving an ambulance during the bombing of Cardiff. In the trauma of battle Dinky was a calming influence and was a member of the Bicycle Club as was Don.

Don came from Dagenham, in Essex. A member of the Society of Friends, he exhibited the high moral principles and rectitude of his sect. Being an older man his influence on Dinky and myself was so considerable that he and I remained chaste throughout the campaigns.

Of all the characters I met, Cockney George was the most colourful. Born in Lambeth, he grew up to be a milk roundsman whose claim to fame was that he delivered milk to Lambeth Palace, the residence of the Archbishop of Canterbury. He was cheerful and inventive, his cheerfulness knowing no bounds. He had the facility to create apt nicknames for most of us. Already, I was 'Young Niss' and wherever and whenever he saw me, he never failed to use this same greeting:

'Wotcha, Young Niss! How the hell are yer?'

Apart from these talents, he had a will of his own which, without insolence or selfishness, led him into audacious enterprises to achieve his aims.

I met him shortly before our leaving the training centre. After our basic training was over, Cockney George found himself in a draft which included none of the friends he had made. This deprivation he set out to change. In short, he skipped the aforementioned draft and joined ours bound for the 48th Independent Reconnaissance Company. When we arrived it was soon discovered that he was surplus to the establishment and ought not to be there. Treated like an alien, he was accommodated outside of the perimeter fence of the camp in a hastily erected army bell-tent. There, he was fed, remained free of duties and lived like a lord for two or three days. Then, after days of haggling by the higher powers, he was allowed to stay, his aim achieved.

With me, Cockney George was drafted to the 1st Reconnaissance Regiment. He ran into trouble immediately. When Major RR inspected us in shirt sleeve order, George appeared ludicrously dressed, wearing only a vest above his waist. He reported that both his regulation shirts had been stolen. I cringed at the expectation of his being charged for the offence of being improperly dressed. But to everyone's surprise he was ordered to collect two new shirts to be paid for out of his army pay.

On board the *Dunottar Castle*, he elected to be mess orderly and cheerfully remained below deck for the whole of the voyage. When we docked in Algiers, he emerged from below in good spirits although, in comparison with our tanned features, his face was deathly white.

In command of the four remaining Bren carriers were 'Laddie', Freddie, Charlie and 'Dobbsy'. Laddie, in demeanour, was deceptive: he appeared unofficious and placid, but beneath this façade was hidden an adventurous nature. Freddie, a Yorkshireman, was of slim build and conspicuous by his striking, large, deep brown eyes. He was the model professional soldier, ever conscientiously carrying out his duties. Dobbsy, a tall, raw boned Lincolnshire man, and Charlie, from Lancashire, were of opposing nature: Dobbsy the more reticent and Charlie the more garrulous, often reliving past experiences of India and Dunkirk.

The armoured car commanders were Corporal George, 'Foxy' and 'Blackie'. Already, the characteristics of Corporal George have been mentioned. Foxy, in contrast with Corporal George, was an outgoing, cheerful Yorkshireman with an inclination towards women and song. Blackie, whose nickname belies the fact that he had ginger hair, was a regular and the only sergeant in the armoured car sections. He was smart and efficient but of his nature I knew little.

Of some drivers and gunners I have written, already, and of Cockney George and the Bicycle Club. Now, I write of the remainder. 'Harry Boy' and 'Flash' were young conscripts; both came from Yorkshire. Harry Boy was from 'Sheffielt' (Sheffield). Tall and strong, he had been a worker in the firm of Hardy Patent Picks and, like us all, became adept in digging slit trenches but with tools which he may have made himself. Flash was tall and quietly spoken. Both had the steady, stolid characteristics ascribed to Yorkshiremen.

'Old Joe', a veteran, was formerly in the Lancashire Fusiliers and had abandoned his 'foot slogging' for the less demanding duty of riding in a Bren carrier. He was short and fair and smiled often, his face puckering to give a good impression of his sucking a very sour lemon. His driver, 'Arty', came from Walthamstow. As a soccer enthusiast, he was inclined to be garrulous when conversing about his town's famous amateur football club.

'Mick', 'Col', 'Weeksie' and 'Simmo' were from London or the Home Counties. Mick was of average height but with a strong, thick-set body. He lacked nothing in confidence and courage, traits he would exhibit in battle. Col was tall and handsome, 'Dinty' short and wiry. Weeksie and Simmo were durable and pleasant comrades who proved their worth in the campaigns. 'Sandy', the driver of Davy's command Bren carrier, was a long-serving regular soldier who rarely smiled. His face was usually glum, his feelings morose. Like a spouse, he saved his affection for his beloved vehicle which he kept in pristine condition and inviolate from any other driver.

Geordie crews dominated the armoured car sections. Jimmy, Bill, 'Wally', 'Oxy' and Billy, bonded by region and dialect, remained inseparable until the death of Billy. Two regulars and a conscript formed the rest of the crews: 'Tich' and Vic were the only time-serving men who had not been promoted; Glyn, from the Swansea area, was a friendly, likeable conscript.

Above are brief descriptions of a band of men at the outset of their going into battle. But what of the armour which was to take them into battle? It was comprised of eleven vehicles. There were four Humber armoured cars: two light ones of three tons in weight - carrying only Bren guns in their small, open turrets - and two heavier ones of eight tons - in their larger, enclosed turrets were mounted, co-axially, 37mm cannons and Besa machine-guns. Each of the seven Bren gun carriers was armed with a Bren gun, two carried Boyes anti-tank rifles and two carried a two-inch mortar each. All vehicles carried crews of three. One of the seven Bren carriers was designated Troop Headquarters, the troop sergeant riding a motor cycle.

For our vehicles, personification reached its completion. It was decided that each would have a proper name. Sixteen Troop was allocated the initial letter U. It was not the easiest of letters to use but, putting our heads together and making use of the prefix 'un', we produced such names as Unchained, Undaunted, Unparalleled, Unflinching, Unfettered, Unapproachable, Undefeated, Unassailable, Unequalled, Utopia and Ubiquity.

And so to battle.

Four

Mines and Tanks

So, to the rhythmic sound of tracks and the frictional hum of heavy tyres on the metalled roads, the regiment moved ever forward. Soon it had passed through the rear echelons of the First Army and into the range of German Messerschmidt 109 fighter aircraft. At intervals, roadside signs reminded us to keep a strict 200-yard distance between vehicles. Then, as the convoy rolled on, it passed a line of burned out vehicles and a stark notice bearing the words, 'These vehicles did not keep convoy distance'.

Now, crews remained constantly on the alert and prepared for the drill of leaving the vehicles speedily and dashing away some twenty or thirty yards with Bren guns, in an attempt to fire at the enemy aircraft. On two occasions when we left the vehicles, by the time we were ready to open fire, the enemy planes, flying low and at high speed, were disappearing into the distance.

The regiment arrived at Ghadimou, for its final preparations. It was there that Laddie was demoted to the ranks. Paddy, the second in command of the regiment, made a spot check of our vehicles and, on inspection of Laddie's Bren carrier, he found it was not carrying the mandatory amount of reserve petrol. From being a corporal, Laddie became a trooper again: he seemed to take his punishment well.

With the coming of morning, the Regiment began its final journey to positions in the front line close to Medjez El Bab in the Medjerda valley. A day and a night's travelling was in prospect and this appeared not to be to the liking of Tex, our carrier commander. He decided on an audacious ruse to ensure a night's sleep rather than a night of slow, sleepless travel. He ordered

Dinky, our driver, to draw on to the verge and stop. Then, as Davy the troop commander passed by, Tex gesticulated and pointed to the engine, signalling falsely that it had broken down. We watched the rest of the convoy roll by and then, under the guidance of Tex, we found a suitable place to sleep. At dawn we rose, at which time Tex took it upon himself to drive, so, at hair-raising and breakneck speed, we careered along the roads until, just before noon, we caught up with the slow moving convoy.

Later that day, on 'Recce' Ridge, C Squadron entered the front line. It was early in the March of 1943. The winter rains had given way to the warm Tunisian sunshine. The Medjerda valley below the ridge was turning green. An unwarlike peace prevailed as we effected the relief of a squadron of the 56th Reconnaissance Regiment.

Its men were ready for rest. The 56th had been in constant action since the 'Torch' landings in November 1942. They had fought in the appalling conditions of winter rains and the morale-sapping mud. They seemed more than ready to go and with speed they went, leaving us in possession of Recce Ridge; to rue the chance of our learning something of their battle experiences.

We settled down into their slit trenches to await orders. The atmosphere of peace persisted until, from behind, came a single, startling rifle shot. We were mystified until John Bill appeared at the back of us, dragging the carcass of a stray pig which he had killed to supplement our rations.

Night came and we mounted our first patrol. Our section of Bren gun carriers descended into the valley, passed through a road block manned by infantry of the Northamptonshire Regiment, and set off into the darkness. Our objective: to find out if Medjez El Bab railway station was occupied by the enemy. It was found to be clear and we returned weary with tension and the strain of driving, peering and keeping the vehicles together in the enveloping darkness.

With the coming of daylight there were new orders. With all speed, C Squadron was to travel southwards to the Maktar-Pichon sector in order to carry out a reconnaissance in front of the advancing 1st Free French Division.

Sixteen Troop was selected to spearhead the squadron and we prepared hastily, while, with disappointment and reluctance, John

Bill buried the carcass of the pig. No longer could we have thoughts of or savour roast pork.

Our journey south ended when we joined the Free French in their outpost line. They were bearded Colonial troops who had made the long march from Chad in the heart of Africa. Somewhat bedraggled in appearance, they seemed poorly equipped in transport and arms: horses were being used; for arms they carried outdated rifles and were desperately short of ammunition for them.

Before our sally into the unknown came a sobering reminder of the perils ahead. To our front, we heard the sound of an explosion and came across the first battle casualty: a French Colonial horseman, riding on land adjacent to the track, had triggered off a Teller mine sown in an unmarked minefield. His horse was killed instantly and lay mangled and mutilated. The soldier lay dying in the arms of his comrades. Soberly, we passed by.

As we prepared to move beyond friendly territory, the French Commander gave us the services of a French-speaking Arab who had been paid to guide us across difficult terrain towards our objective, the village of El Ala. We called him 'Johnny' and presented him with a gas cape to wear as well as taking the precaution of sitting him on the bonnet of the leading light armoured car.

For a few miles, we travelled over flat, dusty semi-desert terrain. Occasionally, we passed hovels out of which emerged dirty, naked children offering both scraggy, almost featherless fowl and eggs comparable in size only to those of pigeons. Further on, at right angles to our path, we came to the first of three *wadis* (dried-up river beds), carved out ten feet below land level. Each had a crossing point where the walls had been broken down into slopes to allow for the passage of vehicles. We paused before crossing to let Johnny Arab converse with a knot of Arabs gathered nearby. He returned with gesticulations towards the crossing and in excited French warned that it was mined.

A search was mounted. Bayonets of the drivers, the only ones armed with rifles, were handed out. On our knees we formed a line along the width of the *wadi*. In unison, the prodding began. In co-ordination, the line advanced. On the shout of 'mine', all prodding and movement ceased. It was then that the brave Mick, without thoughts of self-preservation, began his task: check for booby-trap wire – if none, remove detonator and render mine safe – wait for next call of 'mine' – carry out same drill again.

In all, ten mines were found, defused and lifted. We loaded them into our Bren carriers rather than leave them. We were not sure that they would not be laid again by untrustworthy Arabs and so endanger lives in the remainder of the squadron which was following a day's journey behind.

The delay at the *wadi* and our slow progress in difficult country frustrated our efforts to advance. Eventually, we came to another *wadi* where more Arabs awaited our crossing. Their excitement caused us to be suspicious and not without foundation, for Johnny Arab, after meeting with them, came back to announce that there were more mines. Again we carried out our drill and ten more mines were recovered and loaded.

A further advance over soft, sandy ground brought us to a third *wadi*. This time, a much larger group of Arabs, men and children, had gathered to watch the fun. Because of German thoroughness, in our search for the mines, we expected to find ten, but found only nine. Worried by the delay and our inability to find the tenth mine, Davy decided that, because of its generous under-body clearance, an eight-ton armoured car would lead us across the *wadi*. *Ubiquity* was chosen and Jimmy, its driver, drove slowly across. Then came the explosion. *Ubiquity*'s offside wheel had found the mine. Eleven pounds of Tolite had exploded. Out of a cloud of dust, cartwheeling away, came the heavy wheel. We waited anxiously for Jimmy to emerge. He climbed out unhurt, through a side door, surveyed the damage and then, hands on hips, he uttered loudly, 'The b–g—'s broken my wing mirror.'

But the mine had caused a casualty. Among the watching Arabs, one had sustained a neck wound from a mine fragment. John Bill bound the injury with a field dressing upon which, with a wailing retinue of children behind, the wounded Arab sped off into the deserted countryside.

We left Corporal George and his crew with the damaged *Ubiquity* and set off again. The terrain became rugged and more inhospitable. Rocky outcrops reduced our advance to a crawl. Night fell without warning and Davy decided to call a halt. Having as yet made no contact with the enemy, we 'laagered'.

Guards were doubled. Noise and movement were restricted as those off duty snatched whatever sleep they could. The night passed with only one incident. In the moonlight, a guard surprised a desert Arab groping in the back compartment of a Bren carrier. With a rifle aimed at his body, he dashed off empty handed into the darkness, spared of a death-dealing bullet because the sound of the rifle shot could have revealed our presence.

By noon of the next day we had arrived in sight of El Ala. It seemed deserted and quiet, an ominous portent. Davy decided not to enter until we had created a defensive position. Our slow advance in low gears had drained our petrol tanks to the last half-gallon. More than that, we were very short of water so it was important to lie low and await the arrival of the rest of the squadron.

Close to El Ala, we found a patch of land bordered by a hedge of cacti. Inside, we made our 'laager', dug slit trenches and prepared for the night. Just before darkness fell, Davy sent a foot patrol into El Ala, not only to reconnoitre but also to look for a water supply. It returned to report that the village was unoccupied, but that the water in its wells was polluted with the carcasses of goats.

At nightfall, sentries were doubled and noise and movement curtailed. In between guards, we slept fitfully awaiting a dawn which brought immediate alarm. To our front, on a track outside the line of cacti, we heard the sound of a moving vehicle and saw above the top of the hedge three round, bobbing helmets. To our relief, we had made contact with a Jeep patrol of the 34th American Reconnaissance Regiment which, by some hours, we had forestalled in reaching El Ala.

Sixteen Troop remained immobile until, in the afternoon, the remainder of C Squadron arrived with much needed supplies of fuel, food and water. Our role of spearhead was over. Other troops continued patrolling forward. Fifteen Troop made the first contact with the enemy. Its armoured cars came under mortar fire, one eight-ton armoured car receiving a direct hit which cracked the turret hatch and left its occupants with nothing more than headaches.

Excitement was caused when 15 Troop brought back two prisoners - Austrians who, having no stomach to fight on, had given themselves up – to be escorted back to French Divisional Headquarters. Our exploit under the command of the 1st Free French Division ended two days later, when the tanks of the 6th Armoured Division passed through our positions to mount an attack on Pichon.

We returned to the Medjez El Bab sector where the lst British Infantry Division was hotly engaged. C Squadron was ordered to relieve a company of the Royal West Kent Regiment, on Banana Ridge. After its capture, it had become the scene of fierce fighting. The enemy had been loath to lose it and had mounted a strong counter-attack by an elite regiment, the Hermann Goering 'White Horse' Grenadiers. On the morning preceding their afternoon attack, they had been flown from Sicily to Tunis airport and flung into battle in a desperate attempt to retake the Ridge. They had failed, retreated, and left their dead lying on the forward slope, just below the British positions.

The relief of the Royal West Kents began as soon as C Squadron arrived on the reverse slopes of the Ridge. As Harry Boy and I, with our Bren gun, were about to take over one of the forward positions, a Royal West Kent infantryman gave us the following timely advice:

'Whatever you do, keep your bl–dy heads down, Jerry's shit hot on movement.'

We dropped into the most uncomfortable emplacement imaginable. There were the makings of a slit trench where entrenching tools had struggled in vain to penetrate the rocky surface but had succeeded only to carve out a shallow, smooth basin of rock. Having given up the fight against such odds, the occupiers had hastily collected large pieces of loose rock and had built a kind of 'sangar' around the indentation. We crouched as low as we could but Harry Boy, who was tall and heavily built, suffered the most discomfort, having to kneel and bend very low to avoid exposing his upper body to enemy observation.

A few yards below us lay a group of dead 'White Horse' Grenadiers, huge men who were made more monstrous by their already bloated bodies which exuded the sweet stench of human putrefaction.

For about an hour we crouched and peered, untroubled by enemy shelling until, incredulously, from behind us, we heard the sound of clanking tools and saw a party of 16 Troop approaching, bearing picks and spades. As they passed by, they called that they had been sent to bury the dead Germans. A humane task, but one which the enemy could have thought was digging in to strengthen the defences.

No sooner had the digging begun, than the Ridge came under heavy shell fire. Harry Boy and I ducked lower as shrapnel began to strike the rocky wall of the 'sangar' Then we heard the quickening steps of the burial party running for the cover of the reverse slope. With them came the gallant Mick, his strong shoulders bearing, in a fireman's lift, the limp body of Billy.

After the party had disappeared over the brow, Harry Boy and I were left with the falling shells. For a while we crouched low, saying nothing, hoping for respite. Then Harry Boy, in his brusque Sheffield lingo, uttered these tension breaking words:

'Does'ter want a fag, mucker?'

In my state I accepted willingly. He lit two cigarettes, holding both between his lips and we began to smoke. There we were, two crouching figures, heads down; mine, for want of space, down between Harry Boy's large and enveloping thighs, an uncommon and possibly a unique way of smoking a cigarette.

By the time we had finished smoking, the bombardment of the Ridge had ended. Our relief was overdue but as the afternoon wore on, we knew that no one dare come forward during daylight. It was twilight when out of the gloom at our rear came the shadowy figure of a young, anti-tank officer looking for sites for his guns. With shell holes around us, he expressed the view that we had been 'damned' lucky to survive unscathed.

Under cover of darkness, we left the 'sangar' and returned to the reverse slope. We found 16 Troop in low spirits. Billy was dead. A piece of shrapnel had sliced into his jugular artery. For me, our first fatal casualty came as a great shock. My sensitive nature made Billy's death hard to accept, particularly in the light of the earlier sound advice of the Royal West Kent infantryman and I wished that whoever ordered the burial party on to the Ridge had heard the same advice. More than that, my thoughts were for Billy's mother, a widow who had lost her only son.

C Squadron was to spend another night on Banana Ridge. Now, closer to the top of the Ridge better slit trenches had been dug and the only offensive by the enemy was mounted by the dead Germans on the slope below. From them, wafted by the night breeze, came the sickly smell of death, not only to contaminate the air but also to impregnate our clothing. We longed for relief. It came at dawn. Suddenly, behind us, the sky was lit up by numerous flashes, the silence broken by the firing of many guns and the whining of shells overhead. The reliable, dependable 25-pounders, in the hills behind us, had begun a heavy barrage. From across the wide valley, between the gun emplacements and our positions, with great clarity, we could hear the shouted commands which altered as the barrage crept forward. At a range of 14,000 yards the guns ceased, their silence heralding the end of our stay on Banana Ridge.

Casualties had been few but we were surprised to hear that The Canary and his wireless operator had been wounded when visiting his men in their forward positions. He did not return to the regiment and was replaced by Paddy, his second in command, who was to lead us through all our campaigning.

By late afternoon, the regiment was on the move again, its destination Djebel Bou Akouaz, a hill known in military terms as Point 212. Ferocious fighting was taking place there. In particular, depleted by numerous casualties, the 1st Irish Guards of the 24th Guards Brigade were gallantly fending off heavy enemy counter-attacks by both infantry and tanks. B Squadron was given the unpleasant task of supporting the Guardsmen. Both the Irish Guards and their comrades of B Squadron held firm and their actions were later recorded in the following despatch from 24th Guards Brigade Headquarters:

> The men of B Squadron who fought on Point 212 alongside Number 1 Company, 1st Irish Guards, roused the respect of the battalion.
>
> I should particularly like to draw attention to the conspicuous conduct of Sergeant Salt whose unfailing devotion to duty and ardent zeal in shooting down Germans meant that Point 212 was safe.
>
> The whole conduct and fighting ability of 13 Troop deserve and have our unqualified admiration and gratitude.

In the battle on Point 212, the Victoria Cross was awarded to Lance Corporal Kenneally of the Irish Guards and Sergeant Salt of 13 Troop was mentioned in despatches.

Meanwhile, the objective of C Squadron was to gain control of a saddle-like pass known as the Gab Gab Gap, a feature to the right of Point 212.

Throughout the night, the squadron had travelled slowly along road and tracks. In the darkness, with straining eyes and intense concentration, the drivers kept distance and position, aided only by the tiny convoy light at the rear of each vehicle. There were numerous stops and starts and changes of direction. From time to time, Major RR, seated on the bonnet of the leading armoured car, got off to consult with ghostly figures by the roadside. But the convoy appeared to be going round in circles until, at last, just before daybreak, we arrived on a track leading to the Gab Gab Gap. It was on this track that C Squadron began three of its longest and most traumatic days. Longest, because there was no chance of rest for our exhausted bodies. Traumatic, because our lightly armoured squadron encountered not only Teller mines but also, for the first time, the more powerful enemy tanks.

Momentarily our convoy halted. Almost simultaneously, in front of us, we saw two long columns of sparks shoot upwards against the darkened sky. Mines had been struck again, this time with more deadly effect than before.

Ginger, of 15 Troop, was the driver of the leading light armoured car. Seated on the bonnet, Major RR was giving him directions. Allan, 15 Troop's commander, was riding in the turret. Just before daybreak, on the track in front, a Guards Bren carrier approached. Ginger drew over to allow its passage, little knowing that the verge of the track was mined. The near-side wheel activated one which blew the car backwards, only to explode another mine.

We, in 16 Troop, first became aware of what happened in front when, from vehicle to vehicle, a stretcher was passed backwards. On it lay the still form of Major RR, badly wounded because of his bearing the brunt of the first explosion. Allan, in the turret, sustained an arm wound. Ginger, the driver, was deeply shocked and led away. Later, it was learned that he had contracted tuberculosis as a result of his ordeal.

Leaderless, C Squadron remained on the track. With the dawn

came desultory enemy shelling. It was decided that our armour would leave the track and spread out over adjacent land. Slowly Dinky drove *Unassailable* off the track for some 75 yards. Don, driving *Undaunted*, followed in the tracks of *Unassailable*.

As the light of day increased, we saw that we were in a wide valley between two lines of ridged hills. Behind us, in the distance, we could see the gun flashes of the 25-pounders of the 19th Field Regiment. Before us, towards Point 212, we could hear the sounds of battle.

It was not long before we realized with trepidation that we had driven on to an unmarked German minefield, for, from behind us, travelling over the ground at high speed came a Guards Bren carrier. As it passed *Unassailable*, there was a huge explosion. From out of the pall of smoke and dust, flung high by the blast, came the torso of the Guardsman driver. The Guards major, who had been riding in the front compartment, was flung clear. Badly wounded he lay face upwards gurgling and moaning with pain. Two young reinforcement Guards officers who had been riding in the back compartments lay spreadeagled and prostrate on the ground.

Now came my witness of two deeds which tend to go unnoticed and unrewarded in the heat of battle. Compassion marked the first and determination the second. Both actions were brave and courageous.

Dinky, the unflappable, went over to the distressed major, gently turned him over and cradled him in a sitting position, an act which undoubtedly saved his life, for as he swallowed the blood and tissue from his facial wound he was choking to death. Soon, he became quieter and the moaning and gurgling ceased.

Then, incredibly, the two young Guards lieutenants, from being prone and still, rose as one and, in the true Guards tradition, shouldered their satchels and set off on foot to join their hard-pressed comrades in their forward positions where further perils lurked.

Meanwhile, we awaited both for new orders and for our medical officer to arrive. Before his coming, Bent-M came along the track in his 15cwt truck. He got out with a blanket under his arm and asked me if I would help him to collect up the remains of the Guardsman driver. As we were about to start our gruesome task the order came to withdraw immediately. The Germans were mounting an attack with tanks. Dobbsy, a lance-corporal, rushed up to reverse *Unassailable* under my direction. I was to guide her down her track marks so as to avoid detonating a mine. At that moment, Rick, a young sergeant, newly appointed to 16 Troop, gave me an order in the following words:

'You go and back out *Undaunted*, I'll back out *Unassailable*.'

These were fateful words, for, in the instant I rushed to back out *Undaunted*, there was the blast of another explosion. Incredibly, in reversing, *Unassailable* had sprung a mine. From out of the dust and smoke came a pair of bogie wheels and grotesquely, a length of track extended upwards, remaining rigid like a finger pointing defiantly at the enemy. But the old war horse *Unassailable* lay wrecked on her side, her engine silent in her broken body.

Dobbsy, the driver, was flung out sideways but miraculously appeared through the clearing pall with only a cut on the bridge of his nose. Rick was a more serious casualty. In the blast, of which he had taken the full force, his injury was alarming. In a distressed voice, he was calling that he could not see. Cockney George, who was on hand at the time, eased his distress with a half truth, and said, 'It's all right, it's only blood running into your eyes.'

We who could see knew the truth. It seemed to us that he would be blind in both eyes.

Relief came in the person of our medical officer. There was a shot of morphine for the injured major and then he was stretchered away. Rick was led away and Dobbsy was given a dressing for his nose and, with true grit, remained in action.

Dinky, his face blackened with dust, stayed unmoved and rejoined Don and I to make the Bicycle Club complete. Meanwhile, in these crowded minutes, the enemy tanks had debouched into the valley and were moving towards the withdrawing C Squadron. We crowded into Don's *Undaunted*, carrying our possessions which we had snatched from *Unassailable*. Now, at this of all times, as we moved back, we heard the ominous 'slap' of one track denoting that a track pin had worked loose. We stopped to knock it back and secure it with a new split pin. Precious minutes had passed and the German tanks, by the sounds we heard, were still moving forward. So, travelling at speed, *Undaunted*, the last vehicle to

45

withdraw, passed through a screen of the regiment's anti-tank guns. As we went by, plainly we could hear the calm commands of the anti-tank troop sergeant as the guns were trained on the approaching tanks. At an intersection of tracks, we came across Paddy our regimental commander, his light armoured car in full view of the enemy. He directed us to positions among the guns of the 19th Field Regiment. Our task was to stay and fight it out, giving protection for the 25-pounder guns which were being prepared to fire over open sights. A battery sergeant-major, who had a thumb wrapped in a thick, bloody bandage, was moving from gun to gun, encouraging his men, giving further proof of the high quality of leadership.

The advance of the enemy tanks petered out and they began to withdraw from the valley. They were to return on the morrow, being an important factor in the tactics of General Von Arnim. His strategy was to mount punishing armoured attacks against any sign of aggression by the 1st British Infantry Division.

C Squadron 'laagered' for the night on land behind the gun emplacements of the 19th Field Regiment. There we heard that Johnny, second in command of the squadron, had already taken on the role of squadron commander. More than that, he had had a sad and harrowing start in command, when a young replacement officer joined squadron headquarters: he was 'Midge' who was conspicuous not only because of his lack of height but also because of his wearing of jodphurs. He was a dapper little man whom I had met on a wireless course at Riddlesworth Camp. At squadron headquarters he was told that his first task was to dig a slit trench for himself. It was while he was digging that, cruelly, a mortar bomb dropped into his partly dug trench, mortally wounding him.

Johnny shouted for Jacky his driver to cover up Midge's mutilated legs and then go for the doctor. But the courageous Midge had already accepted that he would die and quietly said, 'I don't want the doctor, I want the Padre.' So it was the Padre 'GF' who accompanied Midge on his last ride.

After a momentous and harrowing day, hoping for much-needed sleep, the men of C Squadron lay alongside their armour. But, for some of us, our expectations were unfulfilled. A party was formed to climb a nearby hill and mount a listening watch for the tell-tale squeaks of the tracks of enemy tanks. So, on the summit, we passed the night catnapping and listening. With the dawn and the eastern sunrise we began the second of our three momentous days. It started dramatically when, out of the sun, came the Messerschmidt 109s. We watched as they swooped down to bomb the guns of the 19th Field Regiment. Lying against the hillside, we fired our Bren guns in reply. From below came the concerted fire of Bofor guns and small arms. Bullets streaked upwards towards us and spent shrapnel rained down on us, peppering the hillside.

After the disappearance of the planes, we trudged wearily down the slope, our bodies crying out for sleep. At the 'laager', I fell asleep in a slit trench only to be rudely awakened by Don with the news that C Squadron was to make another attempt to get astride of the Gab Gab Gap in order to complete the task of yesterday.

Soon, we were passing *Unassailable*, her track still rigidly pointing defiantly upwards and, nearby, the wreck of the Guards Bren carrier on the unmarked minefield. The plan was that 14 Troop was to advance on the left of the Gap and we in 16 Troop were to advance on the right. We left our Bren carriers and their drivers in a ravine as we made a dash to the top of the ridge which overlooked the Gap. It was when we were close to the top that the mortar bombs came. They came with a roar like that of an express train rushing through a tunnel, with whistle screaming. They exploded on the lower slope. For the first time we were under fire from Nebelwerfers, the enemies' six-barrelled mortars. Their bombs fell close together and flung up pieces of rock and soil which fell on us as we pressed our bodies against the higher slope. Luckily, none was injured and we began to crawl upwards again. But worse was to follow, for Von Armin's tanks began to make another sortie towards the Gap.

It was Mick who gave the alarm, calling to Davy that 14 Troop, on our left, was withdrawing. Davy shouted an order to withdraw and we began a hasty descent towards the ravine and our vehicles. Suddenly, I felt a blast of air like that of a strong, gusting wind. The Bren gun I was carrying disintegrated and I was left holding only the barrel. As I stooped to gather up the parts, from behind, I heard Old Joe's high pitched shout of alarm:

'Quick! Get into the ravine, he's firing at us!'

I turned momentarily, and saw that 'he' was a Mark 4 German

tank which had reached the ridge we had just left. As we ran, bullets were making little puffs of soil about our feet. Luckily, it seemed that the gunner had not adjusted his aim to fire at a target moving away.

Under cover of the ravine, we reached our Bren carriers. Some of the drivers had made attempts to make a turn in the V-shaped ravine bed, causing one or two to lose a track from the bogie wheels. When I came to *Undaunted*, I threw in the loose parts of the Bren gun only to find that an armour-piercing shell had penetrated from front to back through three thicknesses of armour. On its course, it had ripped to shreds our packs and blankets.

I found Don, our driver, and we decided to leave the ravine and hide in a nearby field of growing maize. A burst of machine-gun fire made us dive for cover. Unfortunately, I found myself lying on a track through the corn. Don called for me to crawl into the corn but I decided to feign death rather than move. I lay very still in the sweltering heat as the battle raged. Time passed slowly. Beneath me the dry soil of the track was soaking up my heavy perspiration, making an ever expanding circle of dampness, darkening the ground around my sweating body.

Meanwhile, the guns of the 19th Field Regiment seemed to be firing at the tanks over open sights. Shells screamed over our heads and we could hear the menacing squeaks of the tracks of enemy tanks in the valley.

Powerless, we lay until mid-afternoon. Then came a decisive stroke in the battle. First, we heard the roar of aircraft engines becoming louder by the second. Then the earth shook violently under our bodies as bombs exploded. We turned on our backs, glanced upwards and saw that the planes which roared overhead were American Mitchell and Boston close support fighter bombers. The enemy tanks were forced to withdraw and their going away brought a silence to the battlefield. I found the temerity to alter my prone position and, crouching, looked up towards the ridge. The enemy tank was still there with its turret askew. It had been knocked out, it seemed, by our friends of the Field Regiment.

It was when we heard the sound of voices that Don and I rose to our feet. We saw, coming towards us, a straggling group of the regiment's anti-tank troop making their way back. We decided we would make our way to C Squadron's 'laager'. But the effects of dehydration must have made us a little disoriented for we made off towards a line of hills on the opposite side of the valley away from the notorious Gab Gab Gap. As we began to climb the slope, suddenly, from behind a fold in the hillside, there emerged a tall, handsome, heavily built sergeant with a ruddy face enhanced by a black, heavy moustache. Sensing our distress, he came to meet us with a water bottle. We both drank liberally of its contents. For me, it was the most refreshing elixir of my life. It brought life to my exhausted body. So, much refreshed, the two of us set off through a defile. We saw, on either side, resting against its walls, Guardsmen of the 2nd Battalion of the Scots Guards. With bayonets fixed, they were waiting to mount a counter attack against any penetration by enemy infantry. Emerging from the defile, we turned left and followed the line of hills. Towards us rushed an anxious officer.

'Are you Loyals?' he asked.

'No, Recce,' we replied.

'Good heavens!' he exclaimed. 'I've lost a company somewhere.'

With these words, somewhat demented, he dashed off the way we had come. Further on, we came across a long-barrelled gun we had not seen before. From its highly delighted crew we learned that it was a new, 17-pounder anti-tank gun of the 81st Anti-tank Regiment. They enthused that it would prove more than a match for any German tank.

As we left the line of hills, we saw the field guns again and knew we were getting close to our 'laager'. Some distance further back we could see a number of burning trucks and when we reached an intersection of tracks, we came across a young, but distressed Guards Officer who was bemoaning the fact that the burning vehicles were those of the 24th Guards Brigade Transport.

At last, we arrived at the 'laager'. Corporals Foxy and George were back, having managed to extricate their armoured cars from the ravine. The rest of our armoured vehicles were still trapped in the ravine below the Gab Gab Gap.

Slowly, on foot, the men of 16 Troop began to return. Two were found to be missing. Jack, a gunner, had been wounded, Weeksie, a driver, had been taken prisoner.

News of the day's events was beginning to reach us. There had been loss of life owing to the tank attack and from mortar fire.

There was a harrowing tale of one man of our three-inch mortar troop. He had been mortally wounded by a shell fired from a tank. Using only words as a gesture of defiance, he was heard to call out the following challenge to an oncoming tank:

'You bastards! Why don't you get out and fight like men?'

It was during the battle that a Carden Lloyd towing vehicle of the anti-tank troop was withdrawing, loaded with troopers, when it received a direct hit from a mortar bomb. All seven troopers inside were killed.

But other stories were told. In the confusion, Weeksie became separated from the rest of 16 Troop. Hidden in the maize, he heard the sound of a tracked vehicle and, to his chagrin, an enemy tank almost ran over him. It stopped and its commander, dropping to the ground from the turret almost stepped on him. Weeksie was taken prisoner and was last seen riding into captivity on the turret of the enemy tank. Hold-on, the commander of 14 Troop, was taken prisoner as well.

It was 14 Troop that made first contact with the German tanks. As they approached the Gap, one of the heavier armoured cars fired a number of 37mm armour-piercing shells at the leading tank only to see them bounce off. The crew of the car deemed it prudent to bale out before the inevitable, powerful shell put the car out of action.

Di, a lance-corporal of 14 Troop, disoriented in the confusion had, unwittingly, walked towards the enemy front lines. As he walked through a field of maize, he came to a clearing in which he found a deserted enemy field kitchen. Ravenous and thirsty, he helped himself to food and water but hearing voices, blatantly, he set off back the way he had come. Eventually, without even a parting shot from the enemy, he found his way to the 'laager'.

Drained of energy, woefully short of sleep, 16 Troop rested. When morning came, there came a call for volunteers to return to the scene of yesterday's battle both to recover our stranded vehicles and to bring back the dead. Dinky and Don joined other drivers to make the attempt. They returned later, having helped bring back the Bren carriers. Deservedly, both were promoted to the rank of corporal. Meanwhile a small party of men from squadron headquarters set off in a 15cwt truck to bring back our fallen comrades. Seven bodies were recovered by nightfall and brought back to await burial. I was sad to hear that Andy, a fellow wireless operator, was one of the dead.

On the following morning, we dug shallow graves on land beside the track. Then, in the afternoon, 'GF', our Padre, conducted the burial service, as solemnly and sadly, in their blanket shrouds, we laid to rest our comrades, marking their graves with white crosses.

Easter came while we remained in our 'laager'. The valley blossomed with a carpet of red poppies but all around us were signs of war, not peace. The spring air carried both the stench of human putrefaction and the harsher, pungent odour of dead, decayed animal flesh. By now, my sense of smell was so heightened that I could detect the difference between human and animal remains. A third smell pervaded the air; that of the ground plants. Bruised by constant shelling, they released a rank, nostril irritating odour.

Good Friday seemed a more solemn day than that of the Christian festival. Sadly, we heard that our medical officer and a Guards medical officer had been killed by shell fire while in consultation behind Point 212. No wonder that 'JG', our new medical officer, when arriving at the Regimental Aid Post, was greeted with the words, 'You're the third one we have had today.'

There was more sadness within 16 Troop. Dick, a lieutenant, had just arrived to become second in command to Davy. He was lying on his camp bed at the side of the command Bren carrier when a stray bullet ricocheted off the vehicle and, by cruel mischance, took the sight of one eye.

While we awaited our next orders to go into battle, the High Command was preparing its final offensive of the Tunisian war.

We were to play our part, a part that will be recounted as the story unfolds.

It was on our move towards the assembly area that Mac, strangely, decided that he would drive *Unassailable 2*. His driving was erratic and at times alarming, so much so that Dinky and I had misgivings concerned with his state of mind. Nevertheless, we passed through the gun positions of the medium howitzers and the gun emplacements of the 25-pounders. Beyond them, we arrived at our assembly point. Here, in a deep valley, we rested and made ready for the dawn attack.

Mac's behaviour was still giving us cause for anxiety. For most of the night he was nowhere to be found and came back only when the guns behind began a continuous, preparatory barrage of El Alamein proportions. The night sky was illuminated with flashes and there was an uninterrupted wailing of shells. Even in the valley, as we lay, the concerted blast of the guns stripped us of our blankets.

Just before dawn, as we prepared to move to our start line, from over the top edge of the valley there came rolling towards us, like a wave, a great sheet of flame followed by a tremendous explosion. In our keyed-up state, we had visions of an enemy secret weapon.

But, soon, we left the shelter of the valley to join a track which led to the start line. Alongside our vehicles, on either side, in sections, marched the little men from Nepal, the Gurkhas. On our going into battle with them, we felt both pride and reassurance. As we slowly passed through their marching files, some began to step out of line to shake us by the hand, smile and return our greeting of, 'Good luck, Johnny.'

As we drove on, we came upon an incredible scene and the answer to the earlier flame and explosion. Forty-ton Churchill tanks of the 34th Army Tank Brigade lay scattered about, some on their sides. We were told that during the night, as a prelude for the battle, the Royal Engineers had lifted hundreds of British Mark 4 mines. They had been piled near the intersection of two tracks. There had been no time to remove the detonators. Unfortunately, before dawn, a Churchill tank had struck the edge of the pile and detonated the lot. The explosion had left a gaping hole so wide and so deep as to accommodate several Churchill tanks. As we moved through the bizarre setting, injured tank men were being stretchered away, while we collected our thoughts for the coming battle.

From the start line Davy ordered us into action. We moved forward through a field of maize, flattening the corn as if reaping. To our right, moving steadily forward, in sections, at the double, we saw that the Gurkhas were already on the lower slopes of the three hills. In the light of dawn, we could see the path of enemy tracer bullets and hear the rapid fire of Spandau machine-guns. There was no slowing of the Gurkha attack. Even a last ditch effort by attacking enemy Messerschmidt fighters failed to halt the hillmen's progress.

So far, we had encountered no opposition but, in our surge forward, Davy had mistakenly taken us through all three report lines, a move which had left us not only exposed but also a half-hour ahead of schedule. At the edge of an olive grove, our Bren carriers spread out in line and we began to dig in with haste.

Our first realization of our exposed position came when, from the hills behind us, came bursts of fire from Vickers medium machine guns. The infantry of our own 1st Division had mistaken us for the enemy. We saw Foxy in his light armoured car dash off at great speed to stop the firing.

Meanwhile, Mac, Dinky and I, with pick and shovel, were making inroads into the hard ground. We were down about two feet when a shell burst immediately above us. Like a pack of cards, in line, we fell to the earth. When Dinky and I rose, Mac lay on his back unable to move. I knelt beside him, searching his body for wounds.

'Where are you hit?' I asked anxiously.

His reply was only a murmur. Unable to speak, his eyes were turned upwards and motionless. Then, lifting his head, I found massive injury to both skull and brain. A ball-bearing from the bursting shell had made a neat, round hole through his steel helmet; had penetrated the skull behind the ear; had passed through the brain and had emerged at the other side of the skull in a large, jagged hole. Unable to contain the injury with a field dressing, I made a head bandage with the large, yellow, square identification fabric which we usually spread on the ground to warn our own aircraft of our presence.

Mac was dying. He needed aid desperately, but there were no stretchers or bearers to call on for help. While we pondered and worried, we were jolted into action again. From 150 yards to our left, there was a frenzied calling from the command Bren carrier. It was Davy, yelling my name and calling out orders which, because of the distance, I was unable to understand. I dashed closer and heard the call, 'Get the three-inch mortar into action!'

Rushing back, I found the mortar crew arriving. There was no one to give them orders so I told them to get on with the firing.

'But at what range?' they enquired.

Now I realized that I would have to be in command so I ordered them to start at 500 yards range and work up to 1,000 yards. They obeyed without question.

Anxiety concerning the plight of poor Mac remained, and when a gunnery officer of the anti-tank troop came looking for gun sites, I begged him for help in getting Mac back to the Regimental Aid Post. He said he would send a Jeep but such were the demands of battle that the promise never materialized.

Not far to our right, Old Joe was digging furiously when to his great surprise, someone approached his rapidly deepening slit trench and asked for a light for his cigarette. Old Joe looked up from his digging to find a German soldier looking down on him. Having recovered from his shock, Old Joe sent the German over to me. In excellent English, he told me that his mortar had been knocked out of action and that he had come to give himself up. He added that he had played for an amateur football club in Berlin.

So, here was another problem to solve. Both he and Mac had to be got back. In desperation came the idea that we would use *Unassailable 2* as a conveyance. We sat the German prisoner in the commander's front seat and, with the help of the mortar men, gently lifted Mac and lowered him on to the knees of the sitting German. I rested Mac's head against a spare seat cushion which the German held in place. Then, driving as slowly and carefully as he could, Dinky set off with his charges. I was left with my Bren gun and ammunition.

The battle for the three hills had ended. The Gurkhas, swarming over the crests, had achieved their objectives sooner than expected. The road to Tunis lay open for the 7th Armoured Division to exploit.

It was before the Desert Rats mounted their attack that Jonesey, a corporal from 14 Troop, came to take temporary command of the missing *Unassailable 2* and found only a lonely Bren gunner. Soon, he was to tell me that he was ready to kill Germans. In a revengeful mood, he told me that his brother had been killed in action whilst serving with the Liverpool Scottish. I wondered what he would order me to do. Having neither vehicle nor driver, he ordered me to take the Bren gun to the front edge of the olive grove. There I sought and found the most gnarled and thickest olive tree and took up a lying position behind it. I had not been there long when, from behind me, came a great roar of engines. Charging through the grove, in thick clouds of dust, came the Crusader tanks of the Desert Rats. One, travelling at speed, its commander unaware of my presence, directed the tank into the gap between my protective olive tree and the next. More tanks followed and soon they were gone, the dust settled in their wake and the tide of battle rolled on.

I was recalled back to 16 Troop. Fifteen Troop now moved ahead to join the pursuit of the retreating enemy. Its men began to take prisoners, sending back a batch of hardened Afrika Korps men. As they passed our positions, arrogantly, one called in English, 'You've got this far but you'll never take Tunis.'

By afternoon, C Squadron had moved forward a further few miles, meeting Gurkha casualties being carried back on stretchers. We had cause to admire the stoicism of one Gurkha soldier who had horrific injuries to both legs and yet, as he lay with hands clasped behind his head, he calmly smoked a cigarette.

Our forward move ended in the evening. We had reached a wayside building on a rise in the ground. At the side was a burned-out armoured car and, close by, a Churchill tank, hull down, its gun ready to fire. To the right of us were infantry, with their entrenching tools, digging like moles to form a defensive line. When evening came, C Squadron was ordered to withdraw and form a 'laager' about a mile further back.

In our 'laager', we found time to take stock of the day's happenings. Dinky, having rejoined 16 Troop, brought the news of Mac's death, a sad event although we knew that it was inevitable. At this time, Dinky and I discovered that our newly issued khaki drill shirts were blood stained. Dinky's shirt bore the marks at the front, mine at the back. In the heat of the battle, the blood and flecks of brain had dried without our noticing. More than that, we discovered that *Unassailable 2* had been our life saver. On her off side, in several places on her quarter-inch armour, there were perfectly rounded indentations where the ball bearings from the shell had struck her, any one of which could have sealed the fate of either Dinky or myself.

Nick, a friend of mine from 15 Troop, came to see me. He was full of remorse. He made a confession that, as his troop advanced, he had seen one of the enemy running away and, because of the euphoria and excitement of the pursuit, he had shot the fleeing soldier in the back. Full of regret, he said that the happening would be on his conscience for the rest of his life.

After a night of respite, at dawn, we set off to renew the chase: our objective was the little town of Terbourba, in the Medjerda valley not far from Tunis. We entered to find the town unoccupied. There were neither Germans nor Arabs. There was a small railway station. On its platform, along the whole length, great quantities of lemons were piled high. Close to the station we came across a small, neatly fenced, military cemetery containing both white and black crosses, the graves of German soldiers and those of men of the Hampshire Regiment, casualties of the Regiment's fierce battles in the early months of their arrival in Tunisia.

We entered buildings which had been used by the Germans as storage depots. In one room were German officers' rucksacks containing such toiletries as scented talc, which most of our men thought effeminate. In another room were piles of boxes of condoms which, to some extent, engendered looting. In a third room, we found packages of the now useless armbands bearing, in silver thread, the caption 'Afrika Korps'. These were meant to be worn by Rommel's troops on their triumphant entry into Alexandria, in Egypt.

But the reason for our prospecting of Terbourba was that the bridge over the river had been destroyed and the ford alongside had been mined, one mine having put out of action a Bren carrier attempting to cross. Frustration grew as we awaited for Royal Engineers to lift the mines. Tunis was within striking distance and we had visions of being the first troops to enter the city.

Our hopes were soon dashed. New orders came for the regiment. We were to turn round and speed south to join again the 1st Free French Division advancing towards Zaghouan. So, it was 'Tally

Ho!' for the south. Away we sped, crossing the crowded roads and rear echelons of the First Army. With some difficulty, we reached the French. We knew this because we were hampered by flocks of sheep and goats being driven along, the food for French Colonial troops, to be slaughtered in the traditional Muslim way.

Then we came across groups of women in purdah, the wives of the Ghoums following behind their famed fighting husbands. Eventually, we came to the leading French troops, passing through them to make contact with the retreating enemy. This was soon made by B Squadron which quickly lost an armoured car and, sadly, its commander, a regrettable incident considering enemy resistance was almost at an end. The armoured car had been fired on by Italians manning a captured light American field gun. After the shooting they fled and when we in *Unassailable 2* arrived, we put the 37mm gun in tow and loaded its 60 rounds of ammunition into the Bren carrier with intent to use it if necessary.

Soon it became obvious that the Germans in Von Armin's shrinking Mountain Box, were ready to surrender. Hostilities seemed to have ceased. Paddy sent Long John, B Squadron's commander, to effect the surrender of the German general in the sector facing us. Indignantly, the general said, in no uncertain terms, that he would surrender to no one below his own rank.

Paddy informed the French general of the German general's demand. He just as indignantly replied, 'I'm in no hurry. Let him wait till tomorrow.'

This vacillation was to prove calamitous. Darkness fell and from the German positions came constant flashes, great explosions and numerous fires. The German general, having waited in vain, was expressing his anger by ordering the blowing up of ammunition dumps, the burning of vehicles and, as was found out later, the destroying of the charts of his minefields.

By morning, it became clear that the Afrika Korps was surrendering. All through the day, across the open countryside, the German troops wended their way in long, snake-like processions past our positions. One column, in reasonable marching order, was led by an officer riding in a staff car. We made no attempt to intervene, leaving them to be dealt with by the infantry behind. By evening, the war in Tunisia was over. Over 200,000 enemy troops had surrendered.

Soon, the Regiment reached Enfidaville. From there, it was directed northwards towards Tunis and the Cap Bon peninsular. Eventually, C Squadron entered Hamman Lif, not far from Tunis. Even after the fall of the capital, we were welcomed joyously by French people in general but, in particular, by two enthused and happy English ladies who threw roses into *Unassailable 2*. But, when they looked inside her and saw Dinky and me, they exclaimed incredulously, 'Oh! They're only boys.'

They were not far from the truth for we were both only twenty years old. But the last six weeks had drawn us closer to manhood.

Six

Interlude

On barren land, close to Hamman Lif, the regiment set up a camp. There, we were able to bivouac for the first time since going into action. Conditions remained primitive. There were none of the decencies of an established camp. Water was scarce, being brought to the camp by the regiment's small water trucks. Our crew of three washed and shaved in a canvas bucket only by sharing a part of our limited drinking water. After our ablutions, the water assumed the consistency of soup. There were no latrines so we followed a strict code of hygiene for our defecation. The method used was dig, squat and cover, a discipline in which, with a spade, we walked the mandatory distance away from the camp, dug a hole, squatted and then filled the cavity.

We washed our denim overalls in pure petrol which evaporated quickly leaving its own distinctive odour. Our mess tins we cleansed and scoured with damp sand, rinsing them with as little water as we could from our meagre supply.

It was here, because conditions were far from ideal, that I first became infected with the staphylococcus germ, an affliction which was to plague me for the rest of my service abroad. It manifested itself in crops of boils always covering the forearms. With hindsight, I can say that my harbouring of the germ saved me from a worse fate in the campaigns to come.

At Hamman Lif, we surrendered the booty of the recent battle. We handed over the captured 37mm field gun and its ammunition, a German field kitchen and a BMW motor cycle and side car. We kept our jerricans, which held four gallons of petroleum and were superior in both capacity and design when compared with our own two-gallon screw top cans. Smaller booty such as Luger pistols and Nazi flags were hidden and not declared in the hope that one day they would be souvenirs of battle.

Suddenly our rest was over. We moved southwards to the port of Sousse. From there 1st British Infantry Division was to launch a seaborne attack on the island of Pantellaria. Near to the port, we awaited orders while American flying fortresses heavily bombed the island. The effect of their bombing was such that only the 2nd Infantry Brigade was needed to secure the island. Thankfully, casualties were few and were suffered unluckily only by a group of 66 Royal Engineers, when the landing craft in which they were sailing struck a mine.

Now that the campaigning was over for a while, under Paddy's orders we began to spruce up ourselves and our equipment: overhaul and clean our vehicles and generally become more ordered and regimented. Our two-man bivouacs were arranged in orderly lines and pathways and lined with rounded stones. More than that, we were ordered to collect whitewash from the stores and distinctly whiten the stones marking the pathways. Laddie, still demoted, showed his contempt for the procedure by signposting his pathway with a piece of wood on which he had crudely written, 'Rue de Taurus Excreta'. His superiors, not appreciating his sentiments, charged him with insulting behaviour. For Laddie, this was the last straw. Immediately afterwards he volunteered for the Parachute Regiment, went back to England, and was in action at Arnhem. As his parachute dropped he was hit in the neck but, according to later news, survived to tell the tale.

At the same time I found my name on Regimental Orders. With some trepidation, I reported to the marquee which served as an orderly room. There I found Paddy awaiting me. He told me he was forming an Intelligence section and that I had been recommended by none other than Tex, my former Bren carrier commander. Once again, with extraordinary speed, Tex had been promoted to sergeant in the new section.

I removed all my possessions from 16 Troop lines to Regimental headquarters, but I had not been there for one hour when a furious Davy came marching across. He complained to Paddy that I was a wireless operator he could ill do without. Paddy relented and I made my return journey back to 16 Troop. In the end, my return favoured me for, later, on the Anzio Beach Head, the Intelligence section suffered a lot of casualties.

At Sousse, Weeksie and Hold-on came back, having escaped from captivity. Weeksie recounted his experiences to me. After he was seen carried away on the turret of an enemy tank, he was taken to be interrogated by the Germans and then handed over to the Italians. In Bizerta, a Tunisian port, along with a large group of other prisoners, he was put aboard what he described as a wooden hulk of a ship. Prisoners were confined to the bowels of the ship. Hatches were battened down and conditions soon became appalling. Dysentery spread rapidly and the heat and stench were suffocating. As the ship sailed on, it was attacked by our own fighter planes. After the noise subsided, the prisoners realized that the ship's engine had stopped and the boat was silently drifting. Breaking through the hatches, the prisoners found that the crew had already abandoned ship and that it was drifting close to the shore. In a short space of time it had foundered. Luckily, by this time, the coastal plain near Bizerta had been taken by Allied troops. Freed from captivity, both Weeksie and Hold-on made their way back to the regiment. It was a manifestation of their courage that, having signed a declaration not to take part again in hostilities, they came back.

After Pantellaria was captured, the regiment moved to a camp near Kelebia, a seaside village in the Cap Bon Peninsular. There, throughout the hot, Tunisian summer, on a piece of land between olive groves and patches of maize, C Squadron rested. For hours each day, we cleansed and cooled ourselves, swimming naked in the warm, blue Mediterranean Sea. But, still, we trained for future combat. There were frequent route marches. It was during our marching that Old Joe played his trump card. On every march, he went for about a mile and then refused to go further on account of his claiming to have flat feet. He was given a medical inspection and his protests proved to be right. Soon he left the troop for the less arduous task of guarding prisoners of war.

Just before he left, Old Joe showed me two pages of a book he was writing, the title of which was, *The Reminiscences Of A Browned Off Soldier In Battledress*. I suggested that, in his new role, he may have time to complete his journal.

Arty, the driver of Old Joe's Bren carrier, was loath and sad to see him go, for both had spent much of their leisure time fighting imaginary battles on a miniature battlefield they had constructed in the sand, moving around twigs and odds and ends to represent guns, armour and men.

Paddy, our commanding officer, was more realistic. He planned and had constructed a real assault course on flat land above the beach. It was so realistic that the news got around of its renown and other units and groups from the infantry brigades came to use it.

In the autumn of 1943, the regiment moved down the coast to Nabeul, a dingy, dirty town. The squadrons encamped on a stretch of low-level, barren land between the town and the beach. No sooner had we set up camp than we met resentment and opposition from Arabs who, apart from being pro-German, had an undisguised hatred of the French. In these surroundings, our health seemed at risk, too, for malaria was a particular hazard.

Quickly, we were made aware of Arab hostility when we began to find 'Red Devils' (Italian grenades) scattered and half hidden in the soft, earth tracks around the camp. Cav, a sergeant, became the first casualty, losing a toe when he accidentally put his foot on a Red Devil. A more tragic incident followed when a soldier of the Royal Signals, attached to the regiment, was blown to pieces by a Teller mine, deliberately planted on a pathway leading to some canvas latrines.

Further proof of the pro-German sentiments of the Arabs came just after Ramadan, the month of fasting. On one evening, when C Squadron gave a demonstration of its fire power to units of the Second Infantry Brigade, we fired our weapons out to sea, an action which prompted hostile Arabs to cut all the regiment's lines of communication. Theirs was a mistaken belief that the Germans were attempting to land again.

It was not long before an epidemic of dysentery plagued the Regiment and JG, our medical officer, was hard pressed to contain it. In addition I fell foul of my indwelling germ again. Boils covered both forearms. JG, for all his worries, took me under his care, treating my swollen arms with massive hot fomentations and afterwards hastening the healing of the ensuing cavities with cod liver oil dressings.

For health's sake no one used the beach or swam in the sea. There were no showers to be had but Turkish baths were discovered in Nabeul. Arrangements were made for us to use these facilities on one visit only. There, below street level, in dark, ill-lit caverns, we undressed and sat on stone slabs in great heat. The grime on our skins and in our pores was flushed away in a profusion of sweating.

The proprietors – middle-aged, gaunt, Arab twins – were deathly pale, skeletal and mere skin and bones having spent years in their occupation. For an extra payment, they gave manipulative treatment, twisting our necks and loosening our shoulders. Afterwards, as we emerged again into the bright sunlight, we felt not only cleansed but also invigorated.

The realization that our days of rest were ending came with the news that General Dwight D Eisenhower was to review the 1st British Infantry Division at Hammanet, lower down the coast. Paddy decided his squadrons would march there, so we set off in the heat of the day. On arrival, our khaki drill was sweat stained, our throats were parched and we could only stand at ease in the enervating heat. With the infantry battalions we stood in review order and waited. Then, riding in a Jeep, the Allied commander progressed slowly along the ranks of men.

Afterwards Ike – this tall, rather heavily built man, pasty faced rather than ruddy – mounted a rostrum to take the salute in a march past of regiments. As our regiment marched past, nothing seemed to go right. First, in deference to Paddy but without much taste, the band played *The Wearing Of The Green*. As we marched we were not synchronized with the band and, to add to the confusion, Peter, leading our squadron, gave the command, 'Eyes left' instead of 'Eyes right'. Most of us knowingly disobeyed and turned our eyes right, in time to see the flicker of a smile on Ike's countenance. After the comedy of errors we marched wearily back to Nabeul.

In camp we were told that departure for Italy was imminent but before our going an unexpected decision had to be made by the men of 16 Troop. Davy, our troop commander, called us together and solemnly and grimly asked for our vote of confidence in his leadership, offering to resign his commission if this was not forthcoming. We were taken aback by our being asked to make a decision of such import and could only assume that our senior non-commissioned officers had expressed concern with his leading of the troop. Without discussion or consultation and in view of our limited battle experience, we agreed to continue to serve under his command.

Soon, separated from our armour, we moved to the port of Bizerta. From a marquee, overlooking the harbour and inland plain, we saw a supply base of extraordinary magnitude. It was of no wonder that after darkness fell it was raided by enemy bombers and we, on the hillside, were bombarded by the falling debris from shells of the anti-aircraft defences.

On the morrow, we boarded an infantry landing craft bound for Taranto. Once more, on a crowded ship, common decencies were not observed. Privacy was ignored. For lavatories, there were two toilet seats at the stern, suspended over the sea and open to view. They were reached by a catwalk. Always there was a queue of men watching and waiting their turn. Even the most hardened of us found the experience uncomfortable and humiliating.

As we sailed northwards towards the Italian mainland there was time to look westwards at the shore of Sicily and, under sunny skies, to view Mount Etna, the towering volcano rising high above the coastal plains. After some hours of sailing, we reached the port of Taranto and moored in its busy harbour.

After a night in a transit camp, we boarded a train which took us through Bari and Barletta to our staging camp close to the town of Cerignola. There, we awaited orders to join the 13th Corps of the Eighth Army. Christmas of 1943 was spent living six to a tent. There was no real celebration of the festive season, but the Bicycle Club decided to make a Christmas pudding. We scoured Cerignola for our ingredients and returned with all of them except the vital ingredient of suet. In our ignorance, we forged ahead with our mixing and produced an acceptable concoction. We boiled the mixture in a large, empty, cylindrical meat tin, procured from the cooks. Our means of heating was adopted from that used in the desert, namely an empty tin set in a hole in the ground, filled with sand which was soaked in petrol, ignited and then regularly replenished. After hours of boiling, we prised out the pudding only to find out that it was so rock hard it was uneatable. Giving vent to our feelings, we arranged a football match, kicking around the pudding until it disintegrated. Our only consolation was that, at least, we had tried to infuse a little of the Christmas spirit into our drab and primitive existence.

Here, in camp, we had received General Montgomery's message that he was leaving his beloved Eighth Army to become commander of the 21st Army Group in preparation for the invasion of France.

But, of greater import to us was that important changes were being made by the High Command. We were to be deployed elsewhere. Along with Monty, we left 13th Corps of the Eighth Army to be part of a new plan, which would determine our destiny in the coming five months.

Seven

Slit Trenches and Dug-outs

In the winter of 1943, the Allied advance in Italy had been slowing and had come to a stop before Cassino and the Gustav Line. Early in the December of 1943, to end the deadlock, there had been a plan to mount a seaborne landing on the coast, near to Anzio. The plan had been dropped and then quickly reinstated in mid-December. At the palace, in Caserta, the planning staff of the Allied High Command began a hectic few weeks in order to implement Operation Shingle, a landing on the beaches of Anzio and Nettuno.

The task was to be undertaken by the 6th Corps of the American 5th Army. A British division was asked for by the Corps commander, General Lucas. Because of its Pantellaria experience and its having had a period of rest, 1st British Infantry Division was chosen: its task, to land on 'Peter' beach, to the north of Anzio.

First, the regiment's vehicles were taken to be hastily waterproofed in readiness for the landing. Then, secretly and by night, the men of the regiment crossed the Apennines to the Bay of Naples. There, in Torre Annunziata, nestling under the towering Vesuvius, C Squadron was accommodated in a school bearing the name of Count Ciano.

At the school, we learned of a new course of action and deployment for the landing. Another abbreviation entered our vocabulary: it was LOB (short for Left Out of Battle). One half of each troop would make the landing, the other half would remain in Torre Annunziata. There it would stay until rejoining the troop in June, after the battle of the beach head was over. In 16 Troop, there was much speculation as to who would go and we began to make alarming assumptions that casualties would be so great that the LOBs were kept behind particularly to form the core of a reformed troop. But of the future we were not to know. What we did know was that the Bicycle Club would be split up: Don and I were chosen to go to Anzio; Dinky would remain behind.

More than that, we knew that a selected group of armour and assault troops, named 'Bakerforce' after its commander, would make the initial landing along with the assaulting infantry of the Second Brigade. The task of Bakerforce was to seize and hold a bridge over the River Molletta on the left flank of the landing force. Then the remaining squadrons, reduced to half strength, would be lifted in landing ships as the first 'follow-up' forces.

Aware of our mission, we awaited the call to go. We were given some freedom to arrange our own diversions. The Bicycle Club and Jackie, a friend, climbed the slopes of Vesuvius and found the view over the Bay of Naples more enchanting than the sulphurous fumes of a volcano soon to erupt. The day was bright and the sky cloudless so that the sea and sky seemed to merge and, as we looked towards the Isle of Capri, we experienced the optical illusion of the island appearing above us rather than below.

Under the auspices of the squadron, a trip to the ruins of Pompeii was offered. We jumped at the opportunity, only to find our enthusiasm tempered when we were told we would have to march there and back, a distance of twenty miles or more. Our tour of the ruins added to the plethora of 'foot slogging' and so prolonged the day that we spent the last hour marching in the dark.

In these fleeting days of apprehension, there were some who turned to the drinking of an Italian, cheap, red wine called 'Red Biddy' by the troops; some turned to womanizing and there was no shortage of loose women in the Naples area. Those who indulged in these diversions were usually of the fatalistic view and made use of such sayings as, 'Let us eat, drink and be merry, for tomorrow we die,' or the well-known quotation, 'See Naples and die.'

One of my comrades, normally of a stable and virtuous disposition, told me that he was going to make the most of his time, for he believed that he was not going to survive the coming battle. His premonition sadly became true.

On Saturday 22 January 1944, the news reached us that, at eleven minutes to two in the morning, Operation Shingle had begun. From just off the coast and opposite Peter beach, a rocket ship began a heavy bombardment with a devastating hail of projectiles. Ten minutes later, wireless silence was broken. It was 2.25 a.m. when the 2nd Battalion of the North Staffordshire Regiment reported that it was ashore. It was quickly followed by the 6th Gordon Highlanders and the 1st Loyal North Lancashire Regiment. Very little resistance was being met; few prisoners were taken and some scattered mines were encountered but there was no delay in the surge inland.

Bakerforce, the regiment's striking force, landed successfully and had quickly secured its objective, the bridge over the River Moletta. More than that, a further reconnaissance had penetrated fifteen miles inland without opposition. The element of surprise had been achieved.

Meanwhile, from Torre Annunziata, 16 Troop's battle group was ordered to move down to the port of Castellamare to await embarkation. On our arrival there, it was found that Cockney George had exercised his will again. Although he had been designated an LOB, he had hidden in one of the Bren carriers in order to be with us in the coming fray. When his ruse was discovered after the landing he was ordered back to the relative safety of Torre Annunziata.

By the morning of the 24th, we were ready to board, driving our armour up the ramp and into the confines of an American landing ship. Emblazoned across the ship's bridge were the hyperbolic words *Fastest With Mostest*, as if there was a race to reach the beach head first. Rather, we were part of a carefully planned approach by a convoy of ships. We sailed just before nightfall heading first towards the setting sun. Then, under cover of darkness, the convoy turned sharply northwards for the beach head.

As dawn broke, we rose from our tiered bunks and later made our way to the upper deck. We saw that *Fastest With Mostest* was anchored offshore, opposite to 'X-Ray' beach where the first Americans had landed. Around us it was all hustle and bustle. From liberty ships anchored nearby, the amphibious DUKWs were ferrying supplies to the shore. Later, we learned that these versatile craft, after being modified by extending their width some six inches, were able to carry the 25-pounder guns of the field regiments.

Our being put ashore was delayed considerably. Extracts from my diary serve to tell the story:

> *25 January 1944*: Morning. Approaching land with strong sea and air support. Afternoon. Still waiting to disembark. Enemy fighter bomber raid. Radio controlled glider bombs used. Nothing hit but some near misses. Watched cruiser firing broadsides inland.
>
> *26 January 1944*: Daybreak. Rough seas and an electrical storm. Unable to land. LST 422 on fire. 11 a.m. This same craft smoking and drifting about ten miles away. Another fighter bomber raid. 12 noon. Three more raids, 'Talk about the fleet being lit up'. Ack-ack fire heavy and accurate. Five shot down during afternoon and evening. Seas becoming calmer. Convoy in bay becoming bigger. Able to see land battery in action. Jerry shelling beach at one point. Quiet night by God's grace.
>
> *27 January 1944*: Action stations again. Enemy bomber drops a load on land. On terra firma once more.

Apart from the electrical storm which compounded the difficulty of landing, two other factors may have contributed to the delay. At this time, the harbour at Anzio appeared to be unready to receive large vessels such as liberty ships and LSTs. Peter beach where the British infantry landed was available only to smaller craft.

Eventually, we were put ashore in the following way. Because of a sand bar near to the shore, it was impossible for *Fastest with Mostest* to get close in to disgorge its cargo of vehicles. It remained anchored in deep water. A bold decision was made to offload our armour into the smaller LCAs (Landing Craft Assault) while still in deep water. *Fastest With Mostest* lowered her ramp enough to allow the LCA to guide its lowered ramp into position over that of the LST. Although there was a slight swell the operation was accomplished and, with our armour aboard, we set off for the beach. Almost immediately, there was a fighter bomber raid.

Above us, the sky rapidly became pock marked with the white puffs of the exploding anti-aircraft shells. As they dived to the attack, the enemy fighter bombers released their radio controlled bombs. Then, into the maelstrom came the Spitfires, darting and diving through the flak and engaging in dogfights with the enemy.

The Oerliken guns of our landing craft added to the pandemonium: there were two, mounted one on either side of the bridge. Above the noise, we heard the yells of the captain ordering us to get down between the lines of our armoured vehicles. Crouching there, we awaited the end of the raid. Then, as the planes disappeared, so the guns became silent. All the thumps and crumps, all the whines and wails and the patter of falling shell debris ceased. The LCA continued to move towards the shore until it grated its hull in the shallow water. The ramp was lowered and we drove off into three feet of water. All the armour came ashore safely except *Unparalleled*. Unluckily, she found a depression into which she sank and lost power. Almost immediately, she was dragged ashore by a bulldozer, already on stand-by for such an accident.

With the ground once more beneath our tracks and wheels, we passed through Nettuno and Anzio until we entered 1st Division's area of operations on the left of the beach head. There we staged for the night, sleeping fully dressed, each wrapped in his blanket or taking turns of guard duty. On the morrow, orders were received that C Squadron was to relieve a combat team of United States Rangers which was some ten or more miles inland. Those of us in the Bren carrier section were to take on the role of infantrymen.

Our move forward came after dark and we arrived in the forward positions of the 4th United States Rangers shortly before midnight. They had reached the line of a lateral road along which, at intervals, were small farm holdings. There, the Bren carrier crews of 16 Troop on the extreme left of C Squadron were to hold two of the farmhouses and the land between. From a few hundred yards behind, the armoured car section was to provide covering fire in order to give some depth to our defence. But C Squadron was not only perilously thin in numbers but also had to hold a front formerly held by a full Ranger battalion.

With our Bren gun, Bushy and I relieved two Rangers in a foxhole at the edge of the road. Two large figures unfolded and emerged from its confines, proclaiming their departure with these words:

'OK, buddies, it's all yours.'

With this greeting they were gone and we dropped into a foxhole only shallowly dug and almost as wide as it was long. Straw from the farm had been strewn on the bottom. Quickly we realized that it was in a most unsatisfactory position at the edge of the road. By day, it would be impossible to leave without being observed. With this thought in mind, I took a walk to the rear in the darkness. Fifty yards behind, I found a drainage ditch running parallel to the road and stretching a considerable distance. When 'Bud', the troop's second in command, made his round, I pointed out our predicament. Consequently, before morning light 'Bushy' and I had moved back to the ditch and dug a slit trench into its side.

On the following evening, Davy, who had established his troop headquarters in one of the farms, sent for me. In a darkened bedroom, I was given a tommy-gun and told that I was to go with a mine-laying party of 17 Troop, to give cover as it worked at its task of mining a bridge a few hundred yards beyond the front line. We sallied forth into the darkness, the assault troopers with their picks, shovels and boxes of mines, I with my loaded tommy-gun. At the bridge, I went forward and lay in a prone, covering position. From behind me came the clash of picks on the tarmacadamed surface of the bridge. As the noise resounded in the silence of the night, with every stroke I winced, fearing an immediate response from the enemy. Eventually, the mine-layers gave up the struggle to make holes and left primed anti-tank mines uncovered on the bridge. I was recalled and picked my way through the mines. Then, to finish off the night's work, the party laid more mines across the lateral road to the left of 16 Troop's position.

So far, there had been little enemy action except that, after dark, from the wood to our front, an enemy self-propelled gun opened fire. There were brilliant flashes and the noise of the gun echoed and re-echoed all around us. It seemed so near, but it was targeting the rear echelons. After its firing of a salvo, we heard the squeaking of tracks as it moved away, making it impossible for us to take a flash bearing.

Several days passed and there was still no hint of our moving. Poorly equipped for defence, we had dug slit trenches but lacked sandbags, concertina barbed wire and angle irons. Unable to build strong points, we felt isolated and vulnerable. The weather was foul and fickle. On some days, we were drenched by heavy winter rains. On others, under clear night skies, it was bitterly cold. In the night watches, we huddled under capes coated with rime.

On one clear, cold, frosty evening, Bud, second in command of 16 Troop, was making his rounds of the slit trenches. For a while, he joined me on my watch, taking over while I took two hours' break. When he awakened me, behind and to our left, the night was noisy with the continuous sounds of the tracks and engines of tanks. In my optimism, I suggested that the Allies would be in Rome on the following day. Bud, in his wisdom, showed a pessimism that proved right in the long run. On the morrow, an attack by the 1st American Armoured Division not only failed to penetrate the forward enemy defences but also it encountered more difficult terrain than expected. It was withdrawn.

Then, one dark and cloudy night, Sandy, the troop commander's driver, managed to bring up his Bren carrier and with it my number 19 wireless set. Thankfully, I was able to resume my duties as a wireless operator. Because of the bare, flat terrain I hid the vehicle behind a haystack and dug myself a slit trench alongside.

Sandy had brought up a reinforcement operator to assist me in the long wireless watches. He was a gangling, bespectacled, young Jew with a bent for writing verse rather than learning the art of a front-line soldier. Because of his literary pastime, I nicknamed him 'The Poet'. His naïvety and inexperience caused me much anxiety. I set him the task of taking a spare number 18 wireless set to 15 Troop on our right. I pointed out that he must follow the drainage ditch to avoid being seen. He set off on his mission. Soon, to my chagrin, every observation post in the vicinity was reporting that a strange, stooping figure, in a steel helmet, wearing a cape and carrying a bulky object was crossing open land in full view of the enemy. The Poet had decided that the shortest distance between two points was a straight line. He arrived back not unduly worried about his performance and the rumpus he had caused. As for me, I vented my anger in no uncertain terms.

At ten in the evening, for two hours, he took over the wireless watch. I warned him of the need to speak softly into the microphone because of the nearness of the enemy. I got into the slit trench for two hours' nap. I was not to enjoy my brief respite, for I was awakened by the sound of a loud voice enunciating the Troop's call sign:

'Hello! Three Able. Hello! Three Able. Receiving you strength five, Over!'

Clearly, my earlier advice had not broken through the barrier of poetic thought.

The aberrations of The Poet were not the only worries we shared. The farm house which was Don's left-hand position, had an occupant; a grisly old farmer who was adamant he was not going to leave the farm come what may. Apart from feeding him, we kept track of his movements. We insisted that he was to remain out of sight of the enemy. We had to be watchful and careful not to reveal our position and our weakness in numbers.

To give an impression of strength, Paddy formed his three assault troops into an assault squadron with orders to operate aggressively in front of our defences. Several incursions into a wood to our front were made, causing disruption and alarm in the rapidly growing enemy dispositions.

On one of these forays, 'Mac', 17 Troop's doughty and spirited commander, distinguished himself by single-handedly destroying a troublesome Spandau machine-gun holed up in a house behind the wood. Mac had run forward firing a Bren gun from the hip and, on reaching the house, had dropped hand-grenades through the window from which the enemy were firing. At once, the Spandau was silenced. For his bravery, Mac was awarded the Military Cross.

Away to our left, fierce battles were raging. The 24th Guards Brigade, astride the Anzio–Albano road, had boldly secured both the hamlet of Carroceto and the collective farming centre of Aprilia which British troops, in derogatory terms, called 'The Factory'.

The 3rd Infantry Brigade, the only reserve of the 1st Division's commander, General Penney, was now committed to battle in order to maintain a forward momentum. Attacking from its start line beyond The Factory, the brigade advanced on to its objectives; the Campoleone railway station and the Osteriaccia crossroads beyond. There followed some of the most vicious fighting of the Italian Campaign.

Valiant efforts by the battalions of Third Brigade – the Duke's, the Foresters and the Kislis – failed to secure the objectives. Horrifying casualties were incurred and the battered battalions began to cede their bitterly won gains. At the apex of a vulnerable, finger-like salient, they found themselves isolated by strong pincer-like infiltrations of enemy troops, breaking through both the 24th Guards Brigade and the 2nd Infantry Brigade guarding the flanks.

The desperate situation was relieved only by a determined and successful counter-attack by a battalion of the London Scottish of the newly arrived 168 Infantry Brigade of 56th London Division. The depleted remainder of 3rd Infantry Brigade was able to extricate itself and eventually gain the relative safety of the Padiglione woodlands.

Now, sooner rather than later, it became clear that the battle would swing towards C Squadron on the extreme right flank of 1st Infantry Division's front line dispositions. It started with an assault on our morale. Instead of a mortar barrage, the enemy bombarded us with propaganda leaflets. They came by night, in modified mortar bombs which landed in the soft earth with a 'plop' rather than with the usual 'crump' of high explosive. In the subdued light of dawn, we saw that leaflets littered the land around us. Like schoolboys collecting cigarette cards, we competed for their possession and indulged in leaflet swapping. They bore captions and illustrations; some intending to alarm us; some to create divisions between us, the Americans and the Jews; and some to tempt.

One leaflet proclaimed, 'The road to Rome is paved with skulls – will yours be one of them?' It was illustrated with the road from Anzio perspectively receding towards Rome but partly paved with skulls.

Another bore the drawing of a large skull with, inset, sinking ships and ditched Allied planes. Its caption read, 'Anzio! Beach head! Death's head!'

There were leaflets deprecating both Americans and Jews. They informed us that 'Johnny Doughboy' was having a glorious time in good old England with our womenfolk. One illustration bore the caption, 'While you are away' and showed a bedroom scene in which a scantily dressed wife or sweetheart was sitting on a bed as she pulled on her stocking. At a mirror, a glossy haired American GI was adjusting his tie. 'Sam Levy' was also singled out as having a great, cigar-smoking time, allowing the Allies to fight the war while he coined the money.

As the Allies withdrew towards a new Corps defence line, so the leaflets became more directed towards C Squadron in the outpost line. They became more sympathetic and alluring, changing format and becoming free passes to safety. One leaflet, in the form of a pass, contained words inciting us to give up the fight. It read, 'One thousand of your Guardsmen surrendered honourably this morning. Why don't you do the same?' The pass guaranteed safe conduct into captivity. By night, the morale weakening attack continued. As we stood in our slit trenches, we heard a voice which seemed in close proximity. In a mollifying, soft tone, it called, 'Come on, Tommy. You've nothing to lose - only your life. You'll not be harmed if you come now.'

We did not respond to its blandishments but remained silent and still. Jerry had to be kept guessing regarding our weakness in numbers and dispositions.

The morning of 7 February 1944 dawned and with its coming, I realized that I was not well. The staphylococcus germ was on the rampage again. My arms had become covered with large red patches, each containing a small white blister which was the precursor of a boil. Don, who saw my condition, told me to go and see JG, our medical officer, in his regimental aid post, a house about a mile behind the front line. Along with one or two others, I lay in a ditch close by as there was shelling of the area. When I saw JG, I was told that I had a temperature, but, because of the large number of casualties passing through the field ambulances to the rear, he was not able to send me back further. I was to go forward again to C Squadron rear headquarters. There, I would have to stay for three days before returning to 16 Troop. JG's decision coupled with Don's cajoling of me to have treatment certainly enabled me to go on to tell this tale.

At C Squadron's rear headquarters, I was put to work sharing the wireless watch. This task gave me access to information concerned with the momentous happenings which were about to occur in C Squadron's outpost line. First, on the evening of 7 February 1944, the three-storey farmhouse which C Squadron's rear headquarters occupied, came under constant and prolonged shell fire from a battery of German 88mm guns. As I maintained wireless watch, I measured the intervals between salvoes on my wireless operator's watch. With typical German thoroughness, each salvo fell at exactly two-minute intervals throughout the night and on the following morning. The heavy shelling portended an attack on C Squadron.

In 16 Troop's forward defensive locality, Don was doing a splendid job on the extreme left. He had made contact with the Royal Berkshire Regiment, who were positioned to the east of The Factory and a quarter of a mile to his left. At intervals, he boldly traversed the huge and perilous gap to clarify that the Royal Berkshires were still in place. To plug the gap, it was decided that, under cover of darkness, a depleted platoon of B Company, the 6th Gordon Highlanders, would position itself around a house between 16 Troop and the Berkshires in order to strengthen the line.

At dawn, on 8 February 1944, the enemy struck, laying down both a smoke screen and heavy mortar fire before attacking in great numbers. Although the thrust of the assault was directed against the Royal Berkshire Regiment, the platoon of the 6th Gordons and 16 Troop were also heavily engaged. Both were overrun by a strong, determined enemy. The left flank of C Squadron was now exposed. 14 and 15 Troops began a slight withdrawal to the bed of the Spaccasassi stream, where they dug in, under cover of the armoured car sections firing from behind.

From their new positions, the remaining men of C Squadron watched as the survivors of 16 Troop were marched away into captivity. Among them, they saw the tall figure of Bud, the second in command of 16 Troop, recognizable by his long trench coat, and John Bill, the troop sergeant, recognizable by his turkey toed gait.

Davy, the troop commander; Freddie, the model soldier; and

Ginger, a recently joined corporal, were dead. Sandy, Davy's driver, and Bushy were wounded. Only Flash, who had been sleeping in a slit trench, had escaped. Hearing the noise of battle all around, he had awakened and, living up to his name, had made a dash away from the scene. As he ran down the drainage ditch, he was fired on by enemy infantry but, luckily, he reached squadron headquarters safely. Greatly shocked, he was sent back to the rear, not to return. The Poet and Don were among those taken prisoner. After the war, Don told me the story of the early hours of captivity which I recount in the following words.

We were marched away from the battle area until we reached a small quarry with a shallow pool within its confines. We were all herded together and made to stand in the water, up to our knees. Spandau machine-guns were positioned round us. I thought it was going to be the end of us all. We remained standing in the icy water for a long time, so long that I could stand no longer. I decided that, come what may, I had to sit down. I sank down into the water but the guards took no action against me.

Then, a truck with trailer was brought to take us away. Before boarding, we were given loaves of black bread, one to be divided between two men. I shared mine with The Poet. Aboard the truck as, hungrily, I began to eat my half of the loaf, I noticed that The Poet wasn't eating. He had hidden his share in a pocket. He told me that he was planning to escape. At a timely moment, he was going to jump from the truck. I warned him that he would be shot by the guard riding at the back of the trailer. But The Poet's plan was to jump when the truck came to an acute bend so that the prisoners riding in the trailer would, momentarily, obscure the view of the guard. That moment came. The Poet jumped but with cruel luck his foot caught the towing bar. He fell under a wheel and was tragically killed.

From Don, I learned that my Bren carrier, hidden by the haystack, had caught fire and was burned out. The blaze not only destroyed my wireless set but also my equipment and belongings. Nevertheless, here, at C Squadron's rear headquarters, thankfully, I was alive, unwounded and free of the prison camp which my surviving comrades eventually reached.

JG had brought his regimental aid post forward into our three-storeyed farmhouse and had set up in an adjacent, ground floor room. I remember well his arrival; a lone figure, walking up the road towards us, stick in hand, wearing his Red Cross armband and carrying his first-aid satchel slung on one shoulder.

He had not long to wait for casualties. They came both from the forward positions and from the immediate area around the farmhouse. The relentless shelling by 88mm German guns continued unabated and JG's aid post became crowded. Some men had sustained manageable wounds but others, because of the severity of their wounds, were in need of more help and care than the aid post could give. JG became anxious about the condition of one or two of his charges and the deep shock they were enduring. Just after noon, he suggested that each of the wounded ought to make a silent prayer.

Then, precisely at three o'clock in the afternoon, after almost twenty hours of bombardment, the enemy barrage ceased. JG lost no time in calling for his regimental aid truck. It came dashing up from the rear. Both walking and stretchered casualties were crowded into its covered, tiny, rear compartment. With relief, we watched JG take his charges away.

Then, a short time later, a single, heavy shell (we thought one of 155mm) crashed through the roof of the farmhouse, penetrated two floors and devastated the evacuated regimental aid post. That there were no wounded there was nothing short of miraculous.

Later the same night, as I was on wireless watch, the door burst open and a wild looking, excited major entered. Armed and with hand-grenades hanging about his person, he demanded that all available headquarters soldiers must arm themselves and follow him. His intention was to try to regain ground lost by 16 Troop. After madly rushing round to muster men, he dashed off into the night. The attack he had hurriedly planned was called off after the force he had assembled was trapped by heavy mortar fire in the bed of the Spaccasassi stream. Casualties were incurred which the beleaguered C Squadron could ill afford to have. After the sortie, the major left to command a battalion of infantry and was almost immediately killed in action.

Meanwhile, 14 and 15 Troop, desperately holding on in their new positions, were receiving splendid support from the 25-pounder guns of the 78th Field Regiment. Paddy, knowing that his men were being hard pressed, asked for closer support from the guns. He was told that he could have it, but that he must expect ten per cent casualties among his forward troops. With marvellous accuracy, the barrage began, repelling an enemy assault without even one casualty being reported. Paddy was elated by the success of the guns and recommended that a Military Cross be awarded to the major who, from his forward observation post, directed the guns. His award was most certainly deserved.

But, still, there were casualties as a result of enemy action. Four troopers, as well as Corporals Jonesey and Thack were killed. Hold-on, 14 Troop's commander, had been badly wounded. As he was stretchered out of the line with a destroyed foot, he was seen to wave and heard to call, 'Goodbye, Recce!'

That was the farewell of another courageous officer of marvellous spirit; one who had been taken prisoner in North Africa; who had escaped and returned to his regiment; and who had come to Anzio to endure such a cruel blow.

For thirteen days, the 1st Reconnaissance Regiment held on while, behind, 6th Corps was hurriedly forming its last defence line centred on that notable landmark, The Flyover Bridge. For C Squadron, now reduced to 48 men, having suffered the loss of five officers and 66 other ranks, there were indications of much-needed relief.

On the morning of 9 February 1944, C Squadron rear headquarters was ordered to withdraw to a position a mile or so further back. It was because I had no vehicle in which to travel that 'Kench', the squadron sergeant-major, asked JG, who had now returned with his medical truck, if I could travel with him. By convention of war, as a combatant, I was debarred and with commendable rectitude JG refused the request. I rode back clinging to the turret of the light armoured wireless car. JG's rejection of the adage, 'All's fair in love and war' had its counterpart in an earlier incident involving a German foot patrol and a British ambulance. It happened when fighting on the beach head was fluid and confused. The enemy patrol stopped the ambulance which had been collecting wounded. Apart from its driver, there was an armed escort who rode alongside him. The officer leading the German patrol, in excellent English, asked, 'What are you carrying?'

'Wounded men,' was the reply.

'Well, get them to hospital as quickly as you can but I am taking your escort prisoner,' ordered the German officer.

On arrival in the new position, C Squadron rear headquarters took possession of a barn while I found myself on wireless watch in the light armoured car. Mid-way through the morning came an urgent message from Johnny, the squadron commander. His anxious voice revealed the serious situation in C Squadron's forward defensive localities. The armoured cars were still in position and providing heavy and sustained covering fire for the Bren carrier crews, but their high rate of supporting fire had taken its toll of their Besa machine guns. The firing springs had lost their power and were not projecting the bullets accurately or far enough.

Johnny, in his message, laid great stress on the urgency of getting replacement springs as quickly as possible. Furthermore, he said that he needed supplies of all kinds of ammunition, including mortar bombs.

I rushed to the barn with Johnny's message. There, I found Kench and his utterly exhausted men in deep sleep on the floor. A part-empty carboy of rum stood beside them and it seemed that they had imbibed some of the spirit before sinking into oblivion. I tried in vain to awaken them into activity, but, with Johnny's orders ringing in my ears, I decided that I had to take action alone. I began to write an inventory of small arms and Besa ammunition, of two- and three-inch mortar bombs, hand-grenades, 37mm cannon shells and underneath, in underlined capitals, I wrote, 'BESA MACHINE-GUN SPRINGS – URGENT!'

I was considering a way of contacting the regimental sergeant-major in charge of supplies, when I heard the sound of an approaching motor cycle. The rider was 'Batch'; lance-corporal and squadron despatch rider. I told him of Johnny's message and that he would have to deliver the inventory to Regimental headquarters. He did not demur and set off instantly. He was not long away, and brought back the much needed Besa machine-gun springs, reporting that a White scout car would be coming later with its load of ammunition.

Because it was imperative that the springs reached Johnny with all speed, I told Batch that he would have to take them forward. After he had gone, I began to reproach myself with the possibility that I had sent him to his death. But, within a short time, the voice of Johnny came over the air. Batch had arrived safely. I felt great relief, although I was summarily admonished by Johnny for having sent Batch on a mission in full view of the enemy. Still, I felt convinced that my reading of the situation demanded the action I took. On the other hand I felt better when the ammunition arrived with a note from the regimental sergeant-major commending me for my prompt action and initiative.

Relief came at last for the 1st Reconnaissance Regiment. Along with C Squadron, A and B Squadrons, having distinguished themselves with both the 24th Guards Brigade and the 3rd Infantry Brigade, were withdrawn into reserve. The time had come for rest and reform. Exhausted and weary, the regiment came back to its designated rear area on the southernmost fringes of the Bosco di Padiglione. Here I rejoined the survivors of 16 Troop. In all we were just seven; the crews of the armoured cars and myself. No praise is too high for the six crew members in their halting of the advance of the German infantry. Their efforts were rewarded. Corporal George was awarded the Distinguished Conduct Medal and both he and Foxy were promoted to the rank of sergeant.

On my rejoining the armoured car section, I was without equipment and deficient in clothing. I was told to re-equip myself from a large pile of equipment which had been brought back and had belonged to our dead. I searched for boots and clothing which would match my shortness of stature. At last, I found some which had belonged to little Alfie of 15 Troop who had been killed earlier in the battle. I felt no compunction in the wearing of the effects of a fallen comrade; indeed, I felt it an honour.

In the days that followed, there was little chance of wholesome rest. The enemy was attacking the Corps defence line and had reduced the beach head to a depth of only seven miles with a perimeter of about fifteen miles. Now everyone was in range of the smallest German artillery pieces and it was a matter of urgency to seek cover under ground. We began to dig dug-outs of the simplest kind. We needed protection not only from persistent shell fire but also from the prevailing inclement weather. There were two serious problems to overcome. One was concerned with the marshy ground and the other with the shortage of roofing material.

The terrain was such that the water table was close to ground level. To dig down below three feet invited flooding. Furthermore, a strong roof would have to be made to bear the weight of a thick layer of surface soil above. But an attacking army does not provide for defensive works; there were no desirable corrugated iron sheets. Lacking them, we turned our attention to the trees around us and began an assault on them with our machetes, depriving some of them of the branches suitable for our purpose. These we laid across our three-foot-deep pits and, without permission, we filched our vehicle tarpaulins to make a waterproof overlay for the logs. As for the soil we had removed, we piled it high over the structure to a depth of two feet. Then, inside our creation, we covered the damp floor with groundsheets. Now, believing ourselves to be relatively safe from flying shrapnel, we prayed that our refuge would not receive a direct hit.

Around us, in similar style, appeared numbers of smooth man-made molehills marking the havens of many men. For nearly four months, they were the 'homes' to which we returned between front-line commitments. Only once did they have to be modified. With the advent of night air raids, and the use by German bombers of butterfly anti-personnel bombs, the dug-outs were so altered as to prevent a bomb landing directly into the pit entrance and creating a swathe of destruction inside.

Being relatively safe, our attention turned to our vehicles. We dug a separate ramped pit down to a depth of three feet at one end. Down the ramp we drove an armoured car (a light car, with engine in front, was driven forward and a heavy car, with engine behind, was driven in reverse) until the engine dropped below ground level. Surplus soil was banked round the pit for further protection. Engines remained serviceable throughout, even though one car suffered damage to its part above ground level. Shrapnel from a heavy calibre shell not only cut through the armour but also cut through the barrel of a Boyes anti-tank rifle strapped inside, relieving us of this out of date weapon.

To maintain good health, we were fed one warm meal of stew each day. Otherwise, we fended off hunger on rations of hard biscuits and bully beef. As for bread, there were more important supplies coming ashore, so it was six weeks before we indulged in bread slices again. Bottles of 'Stella' beer and tins of cigarettes reached us regularly so that the more enterprising of us swapped both commodities for 'ten in one' packs of food, by courtesy of a team of American troops on permanent smokescreen-laying duties.

It was in the rest area that 16 Troop began a slow build-up to full strength again. A few of those who had been left out of battle sailed to join us. Hoggy, a Derbyshire man, became our troop sergeant. Dinky, my friend of the Bicycle Club, and Charlie, both corporals, came to replace some of our lost non-commissioned officers. Several new and untried men came as reinforcements. Ivan, 'Dinty' and Jennings came to help make up the other ranks. A new officer came to lead us. He was a Welshman and before long had acquired the nickname of 'Mad Taff' because of a number of indiscretions. For his batman, he was quick to single out the suitably named Jennings, much to the relief of the rest of us.

With no time to recuperate from our previous action, some of us were soon back in the front line. The enemy was launching more and more determined attacks to breach the Corps defence line. Now the spotlight had fallen on the 1st Battalion of the Loyal North Lancashire Regiment of the 2nd Infantry Brigade. With extraordinary valour, it was remaining firm around the vital Flyover Bridge. Fierce attacks by strong groups of enemy élite regiments had failed to break through. To give some support and to relay information, a Bren carrier section of 16 Troop set off before first light to occupy a house on the lateral road which passed over the Flyover Bridge and which was to the left of 1st Loyals. In our position, we were also able to give further defence in depth behind 168 Brigade of the 56th London Division. Immediately to our front, 2/7th Queen's Regiment had been placed in the *wadis*, those deep ravines branching out like lobster claws towards the Buona Riposa Ridge. The Queen's, like the Loyals, were hanging on grimly to their labyrinthine positions, under intense pressure from the enemy.

When we arrived at the farmhouse, I parked the Bren carrier close up to the rear wall of the house. I then began my wireless watch, passing on Mad Taff's messages and receiving incoming signals. At hand, I have some of the calls made so long ago, my call sign being Three Able.

Three Able to Sunray (Squadron Commander)
Two enemy toads (tanks) supported by some infantry are operating in the area of the Flyover Bridge.
Three Able to Sunray
Front the same as last night. 168 Brigade beat off three attacks.
Three Able to Sunray
We are now under mortar fire.

At this point, I had an altercation with Mad Taff.

I maintained we were under shell fire, not mortar fire. Being the only one outside of the house and crouched inside the Bren carrier, I realized the greater power of the exploding shells as the shrapnel hit the armoured side of the vehicle. Later, Mad Taff corrected his former message which now read,

Three Able to Sunray
Reference last message regarding mortar fire - correction, shell fire.

Of our coming under shell fire, we realized, too late, that it was the result of unexpected movement in front of the farmhouse. There was living in the house a family of Italians; a man, his wife and their child. Before we were made aware, the wife, in the interests of modesty and decency, had paid a visit to an outside toilet which was open to view by the enemy. We decided that the family would have to leave for its own protection. At nightfall, before we returned to the squadron area, with some reluctance from the family, we compelled them to ride to safety in our Bren carriers.

Just before dawn of the next day, we resumed our watch. Mad Taff showed wisdom by moving to another house closer to the Flyover Bridge. From there, for the next two hours, we watched

German shells systematically reduce to ruins our observation house of yesterday.

During the day, Mad Taff had one of his indiscretions. He decided that he would pay a courtesy visit to an officer friend in the forward positions of the 2/7th Queen's Regiment. He took with him one of the newly joined men who, when he came back, reported a hair-raising crawl down ditches and through steep-sided *wadis*, full of tangled undergrowth. Eventually, they arrived outside a roughly constructed dug-out. There, lying on the wet ground, he waited outside while Mad Taff crawled inside for a drink with his friend.

Our third day on the lateral road was uneventful. An exhausted enemy had finally lost the will and power to attack. Henceforth, like 6th Corps, the German forces became defensive. The two battle-weary combatants settled to face each other across a no man's land which varied in depth from about 1,000 yards in open country to only 50 yards in the *wadi* country.

The price of the bloody battles was high. Reorganization and reform within the depleted 1st British Infantry Division was desperately needed at all levels. At the top level, Major General Penney, the divisional commander, had been wounded by shell fire and Major General Templar of 56th London Division had assumed temporary command.

Furthermore, the 24th Guards Brigade, seriously weakened by heavy casualties among all ranks, left the beach head for the Naples area. This splendid brigade never came back to the 1st Division. It was greatly missed. No one could forget the gallantry of its soldiers both in the present and in the past. On the beach head it was reflected in the award of the Victoria Cross to Major Philip Sydney (later the Lord D'Lisle and Dudley), of the 5th Grenadier Guards and, earlier, that awarded in North Africa to Lance-Corporal Kenneally of the 1st Irish Guards, for valour on Point 212.

As a temporary measure, the 1st Division was brought up to strength by the coming of the 18th Motorized Brigade of the 1st Armoured Division, with its three battalions, the Buffs (the Royal East Kent Regiment), the 14th Sherwood Foresters and the Yorkshire Dragoons. They were to remain with the Division until the end of the Anzio Campaign.

So, after fierce battles came stalemate and trench warfare which was reminiscent of the First World War. The 1st Reconnaissance Regiment took its place alongside the infantry in the front-line commitments and night patrolling. For myself, I began to spend more time than I wished in no man's land, as the following chapter will reveal.

Eight

Into No Man's Land

In the rear area, C Squadron was told to prepare for a commitment in the front line. Sixteen Troop was far from being at full strength in numbers, so its troopers were apportioned, temporarily, to other Troops of C Squadron. Simmo and I were posted to 17 Troop, the assault troop. I changed my microphone for a more offensive weapon, the Bren gun. I became one of a section of assault troopers led by Corporal Jack, who was a fearless man with a reputation not only for a language punctuated profusely with expletives but also for a bold leadership bordering on foolhardiness.

It was fortunate that the men of his section were solid, dependable riflemen. There were two inseparables, Buck and Waterhouse, names that sounded more like a comfortable partnership of solicitors rather than a brace of hardened soldiers. Then there was Albie, a Geordie and the one with whom I usually shared a slit trench.

For us action came quickly. The regiment was ordered to relieve the Buffs in their defensive positions east and forward of the Flyover Bridge. Under cover of darkness, on foot, we moved to effect the relief. In pouring rain, we took over the hastily dug, waterlogged slit trenches; the crude, shallow dug-outs; and the knee-deep communication trenches along which, by day, we crawled to avoid being seen. Immediately to our front stretched a newly erected line of barbed wire entanglements protected along their length, we were told, by a belt of mines. Beyond lay no man's land which we found to be wet, level land marked with bomb craters and numerous shell holes. It was criss-crossed with drainage ditches: fertile ground, indeed, not only for crops but also for aggressive night patrols.

From the start of our commitment, Paddy was determined to dominate no man's land in our sector. As darkness fell, his immediate action was to order a reconnaissance patrol of 15 Troop to set off. Two hours later, it returned elated. Two of the enemy, found lying out on a listening patrol, were seized without resistance and spirited away to put an end to their war.

Paddy, encouraged by this patrol's good fortune, on the following night, ordered out yet another patrol, hoping it would emulate 15 Troop's success. A composite patrol from 17 Troop was assembled under the command of Mac, the troop's officer. Our Section, under Corporal Jack, was given the task of leading. We prepared with some trepidation. We knew that the loss of two men on the previous night would make the Germans both highly strung and doubly alert. But, what was most alarming, the night was not only clear and starlit but also a brilliant, full moon was mocking the sun with its intensity of light.

As Jack led us through the wire we felt vulnerable, exposed and eyed by every front-line observer. We moved towards the enemy line, crawling down a muddy ditch. Suddenly, Jack dropped flat. Just behind him, I was quick to follow, as were the rest of the section. In the moonlight, not ten yards away, there were two still figures. One lay behind a machine-gun. The other, in a kneeling position was leaning against the side of the ditch, his free arm supported by an ammunition box. We lay petrified, bracing ourselves for the burst of machine-gun fire which would surely end our lives. No such burst came, nor was there any movement from the figures. After what seemed an eternity, Jack gave the signal to move forward again. We discovered the figures confronting us were two dead German soldiers. They bore no sign of injury and may have been killed by blast. We searched their pockets for items of identification and, with tension mounting, we crawled still further. All at once we knew we had been spotted. In front of us, two red Very lights illuminated still further the already bright no man's land. Ahead of us, we heard the muted 'thump' of firing mortars, immediately followed by the sounds of exploding bombs around us. As we hugged the bottom of the ditch, the acrid smell of burnt cordite wafted into our nostrils. Sooner rather than later, unless we moved, there were going to be casualties. Mac ordered Wheaty, his wireless operator, to report our dilemma.

Paddy, in his command dug-out, had been following our progress with aerial photographs of the sector. He ordered us to withdraw some 200 yards to a drainage ditch parallel with the enemy front line. No sooner were we there than the mortar bombs followed us again. Again Wheaty reported our plight. Then, much to the relief of the patrol, Paddy ordered us back through the wire. Luckily, there was only one injury, a facial wound to one trooper. Our endeavours were not entirely without success. The effects found on the German dead revealed the presence of the 29th Panzer Grenadier Division in the enemy dispositions.

Albie and I returned to our miserable dug-out. In reality, it was a partly roofed-over slit trench, giving little protection from either shelling or bad weather. More than that, the bottom of the trench had become a sump for three inches of icy, muddy water. We spent the few hours before dawn taking turns to crouch under the sheltered part.

The day brought little relief. Because of the enemy's advantage of slightly higher ground, movement was severely restricted. When, at last, night came, and knowing that we would not be on patrol, Albie and I worked all the night long, building a new, more comfortable, less flimsy dug-out where, at least, we could lie and rest our exhausted bodies.

After all these endeavours, there came a change. Paddy decided on a new ploy. Because patrolling was only possible by night, by day he would leave only the scout troops in the front-line positions and withdraw 17 Troop to the squadron rest area. From there sections of the assault troop would be brought up nightly to carry out the patrolling of no man's land. We in Jack's section would continue to be active every other night.

Our turn came round all too soon. Mac took us out on what was called a standing patrol. Our task was to prevent the enemy from entering an abandoned, heavily shelled group of buildings known as Carne Farm. The farm stood about 100 yards in front of the wire protecting the forward scout troops of C Squadron.

Under cover of a cloudy, showery night, we sallied forth into no man's land, walking parallel with the wire towards the farm and the slit trenches we were to man throughout the night. From the enemy positions along the Dead End Road, a Spandau machine-gun was firing. With a noise like a pneumatic drill it fired intermittent bursts, the trajectory marked by tracer bullets; its direction being too far over to endanger us.

As we approached the ruins, we heard a shout from a slit trench behind our wire. It was from Weeksie of 16 Troop. His voice, full of alarm and excitement, warned us that an enemy patrol had infiltrated into the farm and had opened fire with a machine-gun. Mac, who was leading the patrol, dropped quickly on to the soft, wet soil. We, behind, were quick to follow and lay still awaiting orders from Mac. With a hand-grenade ready, he whispered, 'We're going in. I'll sling a grenade into the buildings. Wait for the explosion – then get up and charge!'

Led by Mac, we stormed the ruins only to find there was no sign of the enemy. Weeksie, from his slit trench behind the farm, with his view to the front hidden by it, had wrongly assumed that the earlier Spandau fire had been coming out of the buildings rather than from the enemy's front line.

After the scare, Albie and I began our vigil; a most uncomfortable one. Our slit trench was about 30 yards in front of Carne Farm. Because of heavy rain, it was holding water six inches deep, covering our boots. Its sides of soft, wet soil were beginning to break down even though earlier occupiers had revetted the front edge with sandbags. As the night wore on and the cold water soaked through our boots, we dropped one or two of the supporting sandbags into the trench to raise our saturated feet above the icy-cold water level. Throughout the night, we took turns to listen and watch, with Bren gun at the ready, with our ears straining to hear the tell-tale clank of arms, our eyes staring fixedly to the front, watching for movement. For one alarming moment while Albie dozed, I was convinced that I saw two faces close to the ground about ten yards to the front. Still and tense I watched until, suddenly, the faces disappeared. To this day, I remain uncertain whether what I saw was real or whether it was that my tired brain and overworked eyes had deceived me and I was hallucinating.

The patrol ended without further incident. With stiff limbs and chilled bodies, we returned, our greatcoats heavy with drenching rain, our boots and socks soaked to the skin of our numbed feet. Weary and speechless, we rode back to the rest area. Back in our dugouts, we divested ourselves of wet clothing and equipment and

sought comfort in the warmth of our blankets and in the balm of
sleep.

Two nights later, we were on patrol again. This time on the
least liked of them all – the fighting patrol. Paddy had been asked
by the 2nd North Staffordshire Regiment, on our left, for a patrol
to make a diversionary attack on a house immediately to our
front while the Staffords, in company strength, were later to
launch their attack on a house in their sector.

We were two sections strong and led by Laurie, an unruffled,
experienced captain, who had taken part, already, in a number of
patrols. Armed with a variety of weapons – Bren guns, tommy-
guns, rifles and even a two-inch mortar – we left the protection of
our wire and debouched into no man's land. Crawling and
crouching, we made our way to within a perilously short distance
of the enemy defences. In the gloom, we could see dimly the
façade of the house. Laurie positioned us to await the signal, a
burst of his tommy-gun. Instantly, we began an all weapon assault
on the building. In the few minutes of firing, there was no
response, only a foreboding silence. With part of our ammunition
expended, Laurie, by whispered message, ordered that we withdraw
slightly in order to cover the imminent North Staffords attack.

As we withdrew, enemy Very flares lit up no man's land and the
tell tale 'thumps' heralded a mortar bomb attack. I dropped
quickly into a convenient shell hole as bombs exploded around
me. I felt a sharp sting on my buttock. I moved my thigh and felt
only a wetness but no further pain so I consoled myself that it was
only a piece of spent shrapnel or a stone that had hit me. I lay,
half in and half out of the shell hole, until the barrage ended.
Then, I raised my head and looked about, expecting to see my
comrades in similar shell holes around me, but there was neither
sight nor sound of them. With great fear and trepidation, I
realized that I was alone in no man's land.

My first thoughts were prayerful. I prayed for delivery and
strength to cope with my predicament. After my exhortations, I
was surprised not only by the calmness I felt but also by the
positive thinking which followed. First I decided to dig deeper
into the shell hole. With my bare hands and digging like a mole, I
began to scoop out the soft earth and pile it on the front edge of
my hole. I worked steadily deepening and shaping the pit, knowing

that it was imperative that I got down below ground level before dawn. By then, I would be able to lie low under the nose of the enemy and maybe observe movement. Furthermore, I thought, it may be possible to attract the attention of someone in our front line who would let me through the wire after nightfall.

But, suddenly, full of fear, I stopped digging. There was movement to my front. A figure was crawling towards me. I feared the worst. Then, wondrously, I heard a voice whispering my name. I raised myself and whispered a reply. To my relief, it was Tommy, the corporal in charge of the other section of the patrol. He told me that he had made two attempts to find me and that, after the failure of this try, I was to be posted missing, believed killed.

Tommy led me some distance to the patrol. The men were huddled against the upper sides of a large bomb crater which was half filled with water. I found a place next to Albie. We crouched back to back and I, frozen to the bone, felt the reviving, marvellous warmth of Albie's body temperature seep into my numbed and icy frame.

For the remainder of the night, we waited for the North Staffords' attack to materialize. We had heard the sound of mortar bombs exploding in the direction of the Staffords' sector. Little did we realize that the attack had been called off. Even before they had left their own wire, the Staffords had been caught by the mortar attack, had received heavy casualties and so could not press forward their proposed attack.

Just before dawn, we abandoned the bomb crater, leaving behind the hazards of no man's land and the scout troops behind their defences. In the rest area, after a morning's sleep, I remembered that I had felt something hit my buttock, but when I bared my thigh I found only a patch of blackened skin with a halo of yellow round its rim.

C Squadron's commitment in the front line was almost at an end. On the evening before being relieved, 16 Troop lost Mad Taff. The last reconnaissance patrol was to go out under his command. It fell to the scout troops to find two or three men each for the task. Those chosen were already tired and strained and now, on the point of their being relieved, bemoaned their selection. Jennings, Mad Taff's batman, had no choice but to go. To complete the patrol, a sergeant of 15 Troop joined as second in command. Of those taking part, only Mad Taff, as he chewed gum, seemed buoyant and elated. When the patrol moved out into no man's land, the quiet was disturbed only by the 'resident' Spandau machine-gun, firing on fixed lines.

Jennings now takes up the story.

We had reached a ditch parallel to the enemy's front line along the Dead End Road. I lay beside Mad Taff who, in a whisper, offered me some chewing gum. I accepted his offer only to watch in amazement as he stretched a piece from the wad he was chewing and passed it on to me. Needless to say, I had my scruples and feigned to put it in my mouth. Then I became more astonished and dismayed by Mad Taff's next order to the patrol, in which he gave the order to charge the Spandau machine-gun. What had been designated a reconnaissance patrol was, at a whim, changed to a fighting patrol. The order was given and Mad Taff charged alone and disappeared into the darkness. Now, under command of the sergeant, the bemused patrol could do little else but return and report the incident. The patrol sergeant at once volunteered to go out again and search. After crawling about for a long time, he came back unable to find Mad Taff alive or dead.

The outcome, which became known later, was that the officer had encountered barbed wire entanglements and was wounded, rescued by enemy troops and taken prisoner.

After its relief, the squadron returned to the rest area but there was no chance to relax. We were warned of an impending drop by German parachutists. For two nights, we remained on our guard, foregoing the much needed sleep for cold watchfulness in slit trenches.

More than that, from the front, news had filtered through that the enemy was using a new weapon against our defences. It was 'Goliath', a radio-controlled, miniature tank packed with high explosive. A few were used and failed dismally. Because of the co-ordinated gunfire of Army Group, Royal Artillery, each was destroyed in a welter of shells, long before reaching the Corps defence line.

Then, determined not to allow the Germans to renew their attacks, the Allies turned to a raid by heavy bombers. On a cloudless morning, high above us, we saw the vapour trails of the twin-fuselaged Lockheed Lightning fighters, followed by the roar of approaching bombers. Into view came formations of American Flying Fortresses. As they passed overhead, the enemy reacted with a semi-circular curtain of black puffs of smoke from exploding anti-aircraft shells. Then came the earth tremors as the rear areas of the enemy were pounded by falling bombs. Several Fortresses were hit and spiralled down to earth. The sky above was spotted with multi-coloured parachutes as the crews baled out.

As we looked towards the crescent of smoke made by the German anti-aircraft defences, we became acutely aware of the contracted beach head in which we fought. Behind us, the sea; to our front, an arc of seven German divisions barred our way.

Soon, in closer support, came the Spitfires to attack the forward troops of the enemy. It was by chance that our wireless frequency was close to that of the Spitfire wing making the attacks. Occasionally, we heard the voices of the pilots and listened as one pilot voiced the following challenge:

'OK, Kesselring! Here we come! We ain't no chosen race!'

The message faded as the plane dived to the attack. It was later that we learned, with admiration, that the pilots were American negroes flying British Spitfires.

The heavy raid seemed to have had little effect on the course of the battle. Both antagonists had little desire to continue the battle. It was to be towards the end of May 1944 before 6th Corps would break out of its beach head.

Nine

Respite

The return of C Squadron to the rest area heralded good news for me. I was selected to leave the beach head for a break of five days in Salerno, to the south of Naples. Firstly, because of shelling, came a speedy journey by truck to the port of Anzio; secondly, there was a hasty boarding of an infantry landing craft and, thirdly, a steaming away at high speed to avoid the attention of 'Anzio Archie', a long-range enemy railway gun which, from time to time, from a distance of twenty miles, hurled 210mm shells into the port area.

Once out of range and on the open sea, I became more at ease. For a while, I was free of operational perils and the physical discomforts of the front line. I began to look forward with great anticipation to a short interval of near normality. I yearned not for the high life but for simple pleasures.

My bleary eyes, now more accustomed to darkness rather than light, needed a tonic. My over strained ears, highly tuned to the menacing sounds of warfare, needed the calming influence of more gentle sounds. My body, weary and exhausted, needed to be rejuvenated. Five days of leave could be the panacea.

Spring was now at hand and, as the landing craft sailed southwards, the sun shone and I marvelled at the intense blue of the sea and sky; at the sunlit, peaceful, distant coastline and, as the craft entered the Bay of Naples, at the familiar, dominant, smoking cone of a recently erupted Vesuvius. In Salerno, by way of a welcome, the volcano had laid down a soft, grey carpet of dust in the streets, to a depth of six inches. It was of no doubt a nuisance to the inhabitants but a welcome cushion for my weary feet.

I found my lodgings, a small pension in a back street. I was shown my bedroom which I would occupy with two other soldiers. My bed had fresh, clean sheets between which I would luxuriate for the first time since leaving home, three years before. More than that, not only would I enjoy deep, refreshing sleep but also there would be the added pleasure of rinsing and washing away the accumulated dirt and sweat with unlimited hot water.

In Salerno, there were preparations for Easter and its people were already in festive mood. The churches, especially at night, were lit by myriads of candles, the candlelight enhancing the gilt within. Sacrificial lambs, limp in death, shorn of wool, white of flesh, were exhibited in processions before being carried into the churches.

In the streets could be heard the flowing cadences of the Italian language and, occasionally, the voice of some budding Caruso singing a warm, sun-drenched song of his native land. Already, the sights and sounds were beginning to soothe my anxious soul.

A delightful journey was made along the coastline of the Italian Riviera. With the blue waters of the Gulf of Salerno on one side, the coach followed a twisting road along the lower slopes of steep hills dipping into the sea. At every turn, the landscapes were enchanting and the coastal towns and villages idyllic. The town of Amalfi, facing south and steeped in glowing sunshine, was unforgettable. Above the sandy beach and reached by marble steps was Amalfi's splendid cathedral with its beautiful Byzantine façade and decorative windows. It is of no wonder that the American poet, Henry Longfellow, wrote of Amalfi and its setting, in the following verse:

> Sweet the memory is to me
> Of land beyond the sea,
> Where the waves and the mountains meet.
> Where, amid the mulberry trees
> Sits Amalfi in the heat,
> Bathing ever her white feet
> In the tideless, summer seas.

Not far away, I came across the Emerald Grotto, with its subdued light, its gigantic stalactites and stalagmites and its weird, eroded rock shapes and then, emerging into the brilliant light again, I felt that there were more enchanting views in prospect.

The coach climbed steeply up to the beautiful, quaint town of Ravello. Unfortunately, there was little time to explore its streets and gardens but I was rewarded by the breathtaking panorama of coast and sea. From a cliff edge, I was able to look as far as the jutting Capo d'Orso. Then, as the light mellowed and faded, the coach returned to Salerno and I felt uplifted in spirit by my experience.

All too soon the break was over. In the last few hours before returning to the battlefield, I strolled alone through the dust-covered streets of the town. I wanted a last glimpse of the normality of life there; to wander among an unwarlike people pursuing their daily lives.

Then, a chance meeting disturbed my feelings. For the first time since my arrival I began to feel envious, not of the inhabitants of Salerno but of the base troops who, in proportion, outnumbered greatly those of the front line. My feelings were engendered by a chat with a soldier wearing the badge of the Cheshire Regiment. I assumed that, like myself, he was on leave from the front, but in our conversation he revealed that his battalion, the 30th Cheshires, was a unit formed of older and unfit men, now working on lines of communications duties. I was neither old nor unfit and realized that my situation would remain unalterable and that only through sickness, battle wounds or death could it be changed.

As I overlooked the harbour, I saw the infantry landing craft awaiting to carry me back to the abnormality of the beach head. I felt pangs of fear as I thought of a future fraught with peril. I heard again the noise of gun fire and thought of the primitive, troglodyte existence below ground. But, having boarded the landing craft, I rejoined my Anzio comrades again. Literally and metaphorically, we were 'all in the same boat'. Once more, I was not alone. The brotherhood of the front line was strong enough to temper my fears.

Ten

The Beach Head Spirit

On the beach head, I rejoined a strengthening 16 Troop. A surprise awaited me. Sergeants George and Foxy came with the offer of promotion to the rank of Acting Unpaid Lance-Corporal, I deliberated and then refused to accept the post. Hours of thought in a dark dug-out had given me time to reflect on my previous battle experiences. I was still very much aware of my sensitivity, my impetuousness and the need to control the instinct of self-preservation. For me, their containment was important in order to allay fear. I believed I had found the answer in my present duty of wireless operator and that there was no better task than being wholly committed and concentrated to maintain wireless communication in a regiment which relied so much on it. I remained a Wireless Operator Class 2 and was paid one shilling and nine pence per day extra.

Shortly after my return it was Easter Sunday. GF, our Padre, had made preparations for an Easter service of Holy Communion and sermon. Regardless of danger from the air above and from shelling below, a marquee had been erected among the scanty woodland trees and numerous dug-outs. In the canvas church, I joined the congregation of soldiers for, as a professing Christian, I felt it my duty to attend not only to make my Easter Communion but also to seek strength for the evening to come. C Squadron had received orders to move up to the line for a spell in the reserve positions behind the now infamous Flyover Bridge and its embankment.

As we listened to GF's sermon, the Germans began a concentrated 'stonk' (barrage). It seemed to be falling on the rest area of the 2nd North Staffords, no more than a few hundred yards away. It began to creep nearer and anxiety grew in the marquee. GF sensed the unease and interrupted his discourse to reassure us that we would come to no harm. We faced it out as we listened to the voice of GF above the noise of exploding shells. Faith was justified, Communion was taken and we left unscathed.

Before nightfall, we were ready for the front and assembled on woodland track to await transport. On the other side of the track we saw the horrific effect of the bombardment of the 2nd North Staffords. At the verge, side by side, we counted 27 bodies, stitched up in their blanket shrouds, awaiting burial. We heard later that several of their dug-outs had received direct hits by shells. It was a sad, silent and introspective band of soldiers who boarded the trucks that evening.

On our arrival in the reserve positions, there were changes for the better. With the coming of spring, the winter rains and frost had gone. The ground had dried out, making it easier to deepen the now mud-free communication trenches. Movement was not only less restricted but also hidden from enemy observation. More than that, our spirits became uplifted by the brave and intrepid 'Few'; the pilots of the Army Co-operation, Taylor Auster, high-winged monoplanes. Constantly, they patrolled the front line as 'spotters' for the Allied artillery. Their actions restricted movement and shelling by the enemy and made life more comfortable for us. When they flew, we in the trenches were treated to a live entertainment. When they ventured too close to the enemy front line, they were greeted by the dark puffs of anti-aircraft shells and hurriedly returned to more congenial zones; when they were beset by enemy fighters, they dropped like larks to just above ground level from where they hedge-hopped to safety. No praise was too high for their feats of daring.

Our task of holding the reserve line included the undertaking of patrols for the front-line battalions of the Second Brigade. I was on one such patrol of a dozen men of C Squadron asked for by the 1st Loyal North Lancashire Regiment.

It was another night of bright moonlight as we trudged towards the rear of the Loyals' positions. On turning up a communication trench, the patrol stopped before a dug-out. From out of a narrow opening, an imposing figure emerged; a tall, heavily built man with a thick, dark, military moustache. It was Lieutenant-Colonel

Rimbault, the Loyals' Commanding Officer. In the confinement of the trench he briefed the patrol. He said that he was becoming suspicious of increased night activity by the enemy around a house opposite to the Loyals' positions. He believed that the Germans were either strengthening their defences or preparing to attack. He asked the patrol to provide him with more information. On its evidence he would decide whether to mount a company attack in the hour before dawn.

Led by our troop commander, we began our reconnaissance, moving forward along a narrow sap until, at its end, we found a lone infantryman. He opened up the barbed wire entanglement and, singly, we passed through into no man's land, into the moonlit, stark, shell-pocked ground; a familiar territory with its chequered pattern of drainage ditches.

As 'ditch hogs', rather than hedgehogs, we began to crawl, deviously changing direction either forwards or sideways as the ditches allowed but moving ever nearer towards our objective. In one parallel ditch, we found dug-outs which we checked; crammed into one was a pile of lifeless bodies which, it seemed, because of the earlier fierce fighting, had been denied the respect of a decent burial.

Then we arrived at an intersection of ditches, one parallel to and the other pointing towards the enemy lines. From there, the troop commander and two men were to move forward, crawling over the open ground to make their reconnaissance and then return quickly down the forward pointing ditch. Meanwhile, to provide covering fire, 'Buzz', a stolid corporal of 15 Troop, would arrange the rest of the patrol in an all-round defence of the intersection.

Buzz placed me in a position facing the enemy. It was then, as on previous patrols, I was bedevilled by the lenses of my spectacles reflecting in the moonlight, in the light of flares and in gun flashes. I kept my glasses covered with my hands until Buzz came round. I told him of my problem and he decided to change my position to one that faced our own front line.

As we waited tensely for the return of the reconnaissance patrol, we were alerted by the jangle of metal on metal and, to our consternation, in the moonlight, we saw a large party of the enemy moving towards us over the open ground. A skirmish seemed inevitable. Buzz, in a whispered message, told us not to open fire till he did. Then, all of a sudden, during a barrage of our 25-pounder guns, one shell, in military terms 'a short', fell between us and the enemy party. Instinctively and momentarily, we all ducked under cover of the ditch. When we popped up again, to our amazement, the enemy party had turned and was straggling up the ditch towards its own lines. The stray shell was a life saver not only for the Germans but also for our returning three men. They had spotted the enemy party in the ditch and lay prone, watched the enemy move away and then dashed back over the open ground rather than using the planned route down the ditch. On their approach to the house, they had encountered barbed wire defences where they lay listening to the sounds of digging and watching the movement of men.

Together again, the patrol made its tortuous way back with the information which confirmed Colonel Rimbault's suspicions. He said that he would now have to use Bangalore torpedoes to blow holes in the barbed wire before attacking. He thanked us for our part and we left the Loyals to their coming ordeal while we, exhausted but now less tense, made our way back to our reserve positions and rest.

Our tour of duty in the warmer weather had drawn the dampness from our clothing, coaxed the stiffness from our limbs and oiled our joints. We spent more time in the sunshine and took more interest in the happenings around us. To our left and forward of us, the Flyover Bridge was under frequent shell fire and we saw proof of the supposition that light travels faster than sound. We watched the puffs of exploding shells being followed by the sounds of their approach. I was fascinated by a piece of reinforced concrete hanging down from underneath the Flyover Bridge and hoping each day that an enemy shell would knock it down and restore some tidiness and symmetry to the structure. We knew when the port of Anzio was under fire from 'Anzio Archie', the huge railway-mounted gun. Always the super-charge, which enabled the shell to go on for a further seven miles, went off with an explosive noise over our forward positions.

Because of the care we took to avoid any movement by day, few shells had fallen on our positions. So far, only one of us had been wounded in a bizarre happening. Syd, a squadron wireless operator, when attending to the call of nature, had scrambled into the crude, canvas-walled latrine only to be caught with his trousers down and to feel a piece of flying shrapnel hit him in the shoulder. Drawing up his trousers over his ample, exposed buttocks, he sought shelter, received first aid then left for treatment away from the beach head.

Later, as a result of an indiscretion, we were to receive regular, unwanted attention from a German 88mm battery. 'Jonty', a young replacement trooper, had arrived with the night ration party. Being inexperienced, he was made troop runner, a duty in which he carried messages from the command dug-out to the forward positions. One morning, much to my disgust and anger, he walked, unconcernedly, across open ground with his message. His action aggrieved me to think of the long hours we had spent digging deeper and narrower communication trenches to allow for covered and easy movement. He seemed surprised when I told him, in no uncertain terms, that we should, sooner or later, pay the price of his carelessness.

Within a half-hour, the first ominous signs came. Air bursts (ranging shots exploding directly overhead) portended the coming barrage. We took shelter in our dug-outs as the shelling began. As in previous bombardments, we were less fearful than in the minutes of waiting for the shelling to begin. We had developed a simple formula to calculate how near to us were the falling shells. The more soil which showered down from the roof above, the closer the explosion. Only one near miss disturbed our composure for not only did it cause a hailstorm of soil but also it shook the ground below us and the timbers above.

After the shelling ceased we emerged to examine the effects. Fortunately, only one dug-out, at the side of the command post, received a direct hit. It was unoccupied but, to our dismay, it contained a consignment of mail which was totally destroyed.

In between our tours of duty in the reserve positions, there were short periods in the rest area. However, parties from C Squadron were employed in carrying food to other squadrons in the reserve line. I was on one such party which assembled before nightfall to bear dixies of hot stew to the forward troops. With two men to each dixie, we boarded the waiting 15 cwt trucks and set off along the Anzio-Albano Road until, to avoid enemy observation, the trucks turned suddenly on to a track leading into the Padiglione woodlands. Eventually, they reached an area just beyond the forward gun emplacements of the Royal Artillery Field Regiments. There we stopped to unload our dixies, await darkness and the long 'carry', across open land, to the entrenchments.

As we lay waiting, the 25-pounder guns began a heavy bombardment of enemy positions, while, at the same time, they bombarded our senses. Our eyes were dazzled by continuous gun flashes; our prone bodies swept by blasts of air and our ears assailed by strident commands, the noise of gun fire and the whistling and moaning overhead of passing shells.

Punctuating the cacophony of noise there came another startling but familiar sound, that of the 'resident' Spandau machine-gun, firing on a fixed line. Its bullets cut a swathe through the branches above our heads, clipping the burgeoning leaves of spring and creating an unseasonal 'fall'. Now, after weeks of guessing in slit trenches, we knew the Spandau's target: the opening in the trees from which we were to emerge. Luckily, we knew also that the enemy machine-gun was never able to depress low enough to endanger us.

When the field guns ceased and the harassing Spandau was silent, a great calm and quietness settled over the battlefield. Soon darkness would fall, but from the woods came the sounds of an ever-swelling chorus. Oblivious of man's warring ways, a neap of nightingales, the 'light-winged Dryads' of John Keats' poem were singing 'in full-throated ease'. Under a spell of such purity of sound my thoughts began to 'fade far away' and I quite forgot 'the weariness, the fever, and the fret'. I was transported to the distant countryside of home. Again I heard the pure notes of a solitary blackbird's song; the chuckling of the Clough Stream at Wildboarclough; above it, in my mind's eye, I saw Shuttlingsloe Hill and, on its slopes, the harebells of purest blue, ringing their silent praises of early summer. It was then that, like Keats, I felt 'forlorn' as the jarring order came to move. I was back with the demands of the moment.

Night had fallen and our long haul began. Expectant and hungry troops were awaiting their rapidly cooling stew. Having arrived at the reserve positions and delivered the stew, we waited for the empty dixies. I took shelter in an empty, one man dug-out which bore witness to the earlier fierce fighting and the heavy casualties incurred. Its roof was constructed entirely of surplus rifles, the grim evidence of desperate measures, taken to survive, by hard-pressed infantrymen.

Our carrying duties done, we returned to the rest area where, week by week, there were changes. The build-up of men, equipment and supplies went on unabated, so much so that our immediate area became overcrowded. A regiment of Scottish Horse artillery, with its 4.5 and 5.5 medium howitzers, had deployed its gun emplacements among the numerous dug-outs. What was more and possibly unique in the annals of Artillery, ammunition for the guns came from small, scattered dumps forward of the emplacements rather than from huge, vulnerable dumps well behind the lines.

Recurrently, the guns bombarded distant enemy targets, then it was bedlam let loose. It was of no wonder that JG, our medical officer, told me of a lyrical thought that came constantly to mind. It was:

'All day long, the noise of battle rolled among the mountains, by the winter sea.'

The guns brought the unpleasant prospect of enemy counter-battery fire but this did not deter either the Scottish Horse or ourselves from clearing a space in nearby woodland and making a crude football pitch. There, inter-regimental games were played in defiance of the enemy and his shelling. For our entertainment, Carrol Levis arrived with some of his concert party, 'Stars In Battledress', but only the compère himself paid a brief visit to tell a few bawdy jokes. They went down less well than the visit of an excellent American swing band led by an outstanding conductor whose rhythmical, swinging hips added 'star' quality to the music of his band.

These diversions served only to emphasize the drabness of our primal cave-like existence. In each tiny, crowded dug-out, three men slept, shared three blankets and huddled together for warmth. By day, whenever dug-outs were used either for shelter from inclement weather or for protection from shelling, there was room only to sit and crouch. Spare blankets were draped down the inside walls to prevent our coming into contact with the bare, dank earth. Men washed and shaved in the open, using canvas buckets and it was not till almost the end of beach head life that they had the luxury of visiting a shower unit installed by Royal Engineers.

The enduring of the living conditions, the perils of shelling and nightly bombing raids failed to break the spirit of most men. On the contrary, a durable 'beach head spirit' spread among the troops. They became even more resilient and less intolerant. Selfishness had no part in relationships. Although danger was always at hand, few men indeed found the rigours of battle and beach head life too much of an ordeal. Those who did usually left mysteriously without our being aware of their state of mind. We did not condemn them, for many of us, in the darkest hours, had been close to the condition which the troops called 'Bomb Happy'. Even Harry Boy, the stolid Yorkshireman, when writing to his girlfriend Lil, jokingly, but with a hint of seriousness, had written that his 'muckers' had nicknamed him, 'Bomb Happy Harry'. Of course Lil replied by heading her letter, 'Dear Bomb Happy'. This touch of humour, trifling maybe, was something to be seized upon and helped to uplift spirits.

Even in the rest area, sadness and death were never far away. One morning, in order to have treatment for my boils, I went to JG's regimental aid post. Alongside the dug-out, I saw a body lying on a stretcher. It was sewn into a burial blanket. The body was short of stature and by the tightly blanketed facial features, I recognized that it was Syd, a wireless operator friend of mine. It was another loss of one whom I would call 'the salt of the earth'. Sadly, he had been killed on patrol during the night. Inevitably, he was one of a trickle of casualties sustained both at the front and in the rear areas, in a unique campaign where all including base troops could not avoid danger.

However, soon there were signs that the stalemate was about to end. May had come and the days were invariably sunny. In the clear air, the Alban Hills appeared closer still. In fact, from the reserve positions, we could pick out creamy-white buildings and watch the eight-inch naval shells of a cruiser bursting on the hillside. Furthermore, there was activity behind the Corps defence line. The 5th Infantry Division had arrived and was being deployed on the left of our divisional sector. More American divisions were in place in the right sector of the beach head. A feeling of expectancy spread through the ranks. It seemed that a break-out was in the offing.

As time went by, so we pondered whether our role of reconnaissance would be renewed. Throughout the stalemate, between our infantry commitments, we had rigorously maintained our armoured vehicles. Engines were run regularly, turrets kept fully armed and cannon and machine guns cleaned and oiled. In short, we were ready to move forward into battle.

To our front, the enemy defences were about to crack and the beach head spirit was to surge out and envelop Rome in a mighty wave.

Eleven

The Road To Rome

On the evening of 24 May 1944, the first historic act of the break-out from the beach head was made by B Squadron of our 1st Reconnaissance Regiment. It became part of a composite force named after Paddy, our regimental commander. In support of B Squadron there was a battalion of the 36th United States Combat Engineers, a battery of 25-pounder guns and a troop of American Tank Destroyers. On being detached from 6th Corps, its purpose was to link up with the northward advance of the 2nd American Corps from the south.

B Squadron's armoured cars began to reconnoitre towards and beyond the Mussolini Canal which formed the extreme right flank of the beach head. In the night, as the force advanced, so mines were lifted and demolitions cleared by the combat engineers. At dawn on 25 May 1944, a sergeant of B Squadron's assault troop, on foot and clambering over a demolition blocking the advance, to his surprise and delight, met with a small advance party of American troops. The link up had been achieved. The beach head was no more.

A further advance confirmed the first meeting, for Paddy's force, having reached Highway 7 (*Via Appia*), came face to face with a patrol of the 91st United States Cavalry Regiment.

Between the two groups, there was a zestful hand-shaking and vigorous back-slapping. Then, with a retinue of reporters and cameramen in tow, up came General Mark Clark, the Fifth Army Commander. For posterity, the historic event was recorded; but, for B Squadron, there was more to do than posing for camera shots. With its task completed it left to rejoin the regiment for still more serious encounters in 1st British Division's imminent attack.

With its infantry brigades at full strength again, the division began to exert heavy pressure on the German forces opposite. Determined company attacks were launched over land on which, earlier, heavy casualties had been sustained. Familiar landmarks were regained. After hard fighting, the strongly held Pantoni feature fell. The notorious *wadis*, the Dead End Road and Aprilia (The Factory) were recaptured. More than that, the Buona Riposa Ridge, on which the Guards and the North Staffords fought so valiantly, was recovered.

It was on the Buona Riposa Ridge that we discovered an ingenious German observation post. We stopped in a valley on the escarpment side of the Ridge. It was steep like that of a quarry face. Into its walls, the Germans had burrowed, carving out small rooms containing bunk beds. High up on the Ridge, they had sunk a deep shaft which contained a large panoramic periscope. From the safety of their excavated rooms, they had been able to overlook and command splendid views of the Allied defence lines.

Soon, battle groups of the regiment were committed. Paddy repeated his old ploy and reformed his three assault troops into an assault squadron. With patrols of A Squadron's scout troops, it began to advance astride the disused railway bed, running northwards from Carroceto to the Ardea lateral road. On reaching the road and on a front of 2,000 yards, the assault squadron dug in for the night. It was here that 17 Troop lost Bill, a Section corporal who was killed by enemy fire. In its isolation, the assault squadron was supported splendidly by a battery of 25-pounders of the 19th Field Regiment.

Meanwhile, Paddy had alerted our C Squadron to assemble a dismounted force to move up to support the assault squadron. Fortunately, we were not needed for by the next morning 2nd Infantry Brigade, supported by the tanks of the 46th Royal Tank Regiment, had moved through the Assault Squadron to attack the enemy's Ardea line, his last 'stopgap' defence before the River Tiber.

To the right, B Squadron was employed in keeping contact with the 45th American Division, until, in its surge forward, it began to encroach on 1st Division's sector, forcing it to strike still further north-westwards. B Squadron was obliged to switch rapidly behind 1st Division to its left flank, to be detached to 5th British Division.

The movement forward of 6th American Corps was increasing in momentum. All along its front, attacks were gaining ground. Again on the divisional commander's orders, Paddy was asked to lead another force named a 'Jock Column'. It comprised A and C Squadrons of the regiment, the 14th Battalion, the Sherwood Foresters, two squadrons of the 46th Royal Tank Regiment, a Battery of the 19th Field Regiment, a detachment of 238 Company, Royal Engineers and a troop of the 81st Anti-tank Regiment, the whole under the command of the 18th Motorized Brigade.

On 4 June 1944, in co-ordination with a general advance, C Squadron took on the role of flank protection for Paddy's formidable Force. Progress forward was rapid and sometimes confusing for we found ourselves mingling with advancing American formations, their line of advance squeezing us further still to the north-west. At noon, we swung over to the west and soon, with elation, we reached the banks of the River Tiber. There, we waited for the infantry to concentrate behind us.

On 5 June 1944, Paddy's Force crossed the Tiber. A further pursuit of the enemy began until, eight miles beyond the river, the Force stopped to establish strong points and await the arrival of the infantry.

The morning of 6 June 1944 dawned. As we awaited further orders, there came the momentous news that the Allies were landing on the beaches of Normandy. The long-awaited Second Front had begun. We were told that the capture of Rome, on 5 June, would have been a marvellous fillip for the invaders. For us, there was some relief that we were no longer fighting a lonely, forgotten war. Furthermore, there was relief in the newly found freedom from the restriction of the beach head. We relaxed and waited. Then, from within our 'laager', at the side of the road leading northwards, we heard the sound of vehicles approaching from behind. Down the road came a long convoy of Jeeps, each carrying a section of fully armed men with Oriental faces. It was a battalion of Japanese Americans which sped onwards towards the retreating enemy. Immediately afterwards came the news that we had hoped for. The 1st British Infantry Division was to cease operations. All units were to withdraw for rest after continuous action since 22 January 1944.

The cost of months of heavy fighting was high. The total battle casualties of the division amounted to 8,868 men of all ranks. Its honours and awards were a reflection of the gallantry of its soldiers. One Victoria Cross and 206 other awards were won.

In our own 1st Reconnaissance Regiment, Paddy and Long John were awarded the Distinguished Service Order. In C Squadron, Mac, 17 Troop's commander, won the Military Cross. Corporal George of our own 16 Troop, received the Distinguished Conduct Medal and Corporal SF of 15 Troop was Mentioned In Despatches.

A fitting end to the story or the Anzio Campaign can be found in these extracts from the personal notes of the Commander of the First Division.

After four and a half months, the division emerged from its foxholes and its shelters with high morale and unbroken spirit to prove beyond any shadow of doubt that their experience had in no way impaired their will and ability to pursue and defeat the enemy. They finished north of the Tiber, thus completing their contribution to the liberation of Rome.

Everyone was in it from start to finish, and that in itself engendered a more than ordinary spirit of comradeship and common endeavour. In the cemetery lie representatives of every corps and service - infantry inevitably preponderating; gunners and pioneers; tank crews and cooks; ambulance drivers, medical orderlies and military police; sappers and signallers; sailors and airmen; machine-gunners and mortar men; men of the Reconnaissance Corps, REME and RASC. All played their part and shared the cost.

Twelve

Rome, Florence and the Gothic Line

Four miles south of Rome, with a distant view of The Eternal City, we found our haven. The regiment encamped in the grounds of a requisitioned villa. There, in a grove of trees, between piles of abandoned German 88mm shells, we pitched our two-men bivouacs, our luxury homes after our earlier dank, dark dug-outs. Ivan, one of the replacements, as yet unfamiliar with the impermanence of life in a combat unit and with his mind not yet blunted by the squalor and obscenities of war, aspired to even greater heights of comfort. From debris lying around, he built a tree house. Within this 'love nest', he covertly entertained one of Rome's courtesans.

Unlike Ivan, and knowing our stay would be temporary, we went to no such trouble as reform and retraining continued. Those left out of battle rejoined us from the Naples area. Fresh, young men from the Corps Replacement Unit came in place of those lost in the Anzio Campaign. With their coming, I lost my status as the youngest soldier in the troop. Harry, a Londoner, was given the appendage of 'Young Harry', usurping my position of 'Young Niss'.

Apart from training, there was time for leisure. Opportunities arose for visits to Rome to gaze at and admire the beauty and magnificence of its great buildings - the basilica and dome of St Peter's, the Castel San Angelo, the Vittorio Emmanuele Palace and, great edifice of Rome's glorious past, the Colosseum. It was here, after crossing the thoroughfare opposite, that my friends and I were confronted by a long wall, on which, sculpted in concrete, were large maps emblazoned with patches of red marking the conquests of Mussolini's fascist state which was now another

112

Roman Empire in demise.

On one occasion, I went to the Foro di Italia; a splendid sports stadium, where I watched the Allied Track and Field Championships. Military spectators in sparse groups sat on the warm, stone seating of the huge arena and saw a strong United States military athletics team dominate the events. Here, in more peaceful confrontation, the smaller teams of fighting men from countries across the world were no match for the Americans.

At this time, the Regiment was asked to form a detachment of men to attend a Remembrance Service for the fallen of the 1st British Division in the recent Anzio Campaign. All Saints Church was the chosen venue and I was one of those picked to attend. Afterwards, Paddy, who was present at the ceremony, showed great displeasure at our appearance. We had failed to match up to his exacting standards of smartness, even though, after the Anzio Campaign, we had done our best to smarten up.

On our return, we found the whole camp in a state of excited, almost frenzied hustle and bustle. The news was that, on the morrow, His Majesty King George the Sixth would be reviewing the regiment from a staff car as it passed by on the road outside of the encampment.

With Paddy's earlier reproof fresh in mind and amid feverish cleaning and polishing, I washed my offending khaki drill uniform. In the warm, evening sunlight, I left it to dry. At sunset, only my shorts remained wet, but I was confident that the Italian, summer night would dry them. I slept.

When morning came, to my horror, the shorts were still wet and unfit to wear. There was no way that I could pay my respects to His Majesty while I was wearing wet shorts. Fearing the worst, I went to Hoggy, the troop sergeant, to report my dilemma. With least expected leniency, he ordered me to lie low in my bivouac until the parade was over. With a mixture of disappointment and relief, I stayed and listened to the cheers that marked the King's passing through the ranks. With surprising speed, the formalities were over. My friends returned disappointed that the royal car had neither slowed nor stopped, but, in their fleeting glimpses, they had noticed that the King had looked far from well.

The review by the King was the precursor of our going into action again. In the camp, there were briefings when maps of the front line appeared. The advance of the Allied armies were followed with more interest. By now, the rapidity of the advance had slowed on reaching Kesselring's Arno defence line in front of Florence. Forward divisions were in need of rest. After six weeks of rest, the 1st Infantry Division was ordered to the relief of the 4th Infantry Division operating in the Arno bend, east of Florence.

The journey northwards began in the heat of the Italian summer. It was early in the August of 1944 when our convoy of armoured cars and Bren carriers rolled through the beautiful, Umbrian countryside. Without so much as a pause to admire its beauty, we left behind its picturesque hills and vineyards and its scattered towns and villages. In Tuscany, we reached Foligno, not far from the famous town of Assisi. At Foligno, the regiment staged for its final preparations before entering the front line. It was during this stay that I had occasion to visit the lieutenant quartermaster's regimental store. I was not impressed by what I saw. One of the regimental Pioneers was painting a wooden cross, the last one of fifteen which he said had to be made ready for the coming confrontation with the enemy. Already my equanimity had been jolted by learning that the regimental headquarters cook sewed the dead into blankets, in preparation for burial. I began to feel less envious of the men in the rear echelons of the regiment.

On the next day, the convoy skirted the heat-misted stretch of Lake Trasimeno around which both ancient and recent battles had been fought. The lake and its surrounds were now tranquil but, for me, about to go into the front line, the tranquillity did nothing to allay my apprehension or relieve my tension.

The convoy began to pass through the rear echelons of 13th Corps and, in the turret of an armoured car, I felt envious of the support troops I saw in their workshops, in their supply dumps and in their wayside tented camps. All were going about their multifarious tasks but they were tasks which I knew were essential for the support of the combat soldier.

Steadily, the regiment moved onwards towards the battle zone. Occasionally, there was a glimpse of a howitzer of an artillery medium regiment, a reminder that we were nearing the front line. From forward of us came the distant, ominous, familiar 'pings' of the field regiment's 25-pounder guns in action.

Once we were beyond the guns, we entered that risky,

indeterminate width of land known as the front line. In the late afternoon, quietly and without interference from the enemy, we began to relieve forward troops on the right flank of the divisional sector. We took up positions on the tree-covered slopes of the River Arno valley, to the east of Florence and overlooking the river as it stretched eastwards until it made a great right-angled bend southwards towards Figline and Arezzo.

On the northern bank of the river, close to the point of the bend, lay Pontassieve, an enemy held town. By aggressive patrolling, it was our objective to force the enemy to withdraw from the town. Again, we resorted to the now familiar role of patrolling on foot, for we hardly used our armour except to keep contact with units of the 6th Armoured Division to our right. Nightly patrols were ordered. Daring crossings of the river were made. One patrol, crossing where the water was shallow, entered Pontassieve under cover of darkness and when daylight came, remained holed up in a house in the town, observing movement of enemy troops who were totally unaware of its presence. At nightfall, before recrossing the river, the patrol successfully attacked an enemy observation post.

One of C Squadron's patrols crossed the river to the east of Pontassieve and advanced four miles beyond and in rear of the German dispositions. They engaged the enemy in one clash and, without losing a man, inflicted a number of casualties.

After another skirmish across a railway line, 'Smudger', a corporal of 14 Troop, returned somewhat ill humoured and irate, declaring that he had been hit on a buttock. He was encouraged to drop his torn, blood-stained trousers so that we could look at his injury. We were surprised to see that a heavy calibre bullet had made a neat, U-shaped furrow in the buttock. It was about three inches long and a half inch in depth and width. The bullet had ploughed its way, at a tangent, through the fleshy part of the buttock. The dimensions of the wound suggested that, in the confusion of the night skirmish, it had been inflicted by a tommy-gun. Be that as it may, Smudger's campaigning was over and, grudgingly, he left us, bearing a lasting souvenir of his part in the war.

The pressure exerted by our patrols against the defenders of Pontassieve forced the latter's withdrawal northwards. At the same time, 13th Corps had ordered a regrouping which entailed our moving. 1st British Division was to change places with 8th Indian Division which was deployed opposite Florence and to the south of the River Arno. The clearing of the city became the responsibility of the three infantry brigades of 1st Division.

1st Reconnaissance Regiment moved to take up new positions in that part of Florence, south of the River Arno. Reunited with its armour, C Squadron awaited the building of a pontoon bridge because all other bridges except the famous Ponte Vecchio had been destroyed by the retreating German forces. Even this bridge could not be used, its southern end being blocked by demolitions and mines.

But, once across the river, we took up positions in the northern suburbs of the city. Here, during daylight hours, there was enemy shell fire which did not unduly worry us, the shells exploding mostly on the roofs of buildings.

With the coming of darkness, a nightmarish experience began. Uncertain as we were to the whereabouts of the enemy and disoriented by the darkness, our eyes, ears and nerves were strained to the limit. A sudden burst of Spandau machine-gun fire seemed to come from behind us rather than from the front, arousing fears of infiltration. Exploding shells re-echoed, their explosions reverberating and amplifying in the confined spaces of the streets. Shells that hit roof-tops made balls of fire, creating momentary infernos the like of which we had not seen in daylight shelling.

In between the flashes, the explosions and the machine-gun bursts, an eerie and weird silence prevailed. It was if a stunned and stupefied, personified city was holding its breath while alien forces were breathing fire and destruction into its vitals.

The nerve-racking darkness gave way to a welcome dawn. In the daylight, we relaxed as the battalions of 2nd Infantry Brigade began their advance through the suburbs and into the hills beyond. It was time, too, for the regiment to leave the city, its squadrons being deployed on both flanks of the division. For C Squadron, there was little chance to employ its armour in reconnaissance. It had advanced westwards towards Sesto only to find that the line of advance turned abruptly into the hilly country north-west of Florence. It was time to adopt an infantry role again.

Leaving our vehicles behind, we donned field service marching order. Heavily loaded with arms and equipment, we moved forward and upward to make contact with the enemy. Contact was soon made when a Spandau machine-gun, ensconced in a farm high above us, fired sporadic bursts down a walled, narrow road leading towards us. Half way up the hill stood a small church with a tower. It became C Squadron's objective.

Johnny, our commander, ordered 16 Troop forward to the shelter of a house at the bottom of the hill. There, we quickly divested ourselves of large packs before getting a quick briefing. We were to reach the church by crossing the walled road under fire and then by charging up the hillside to the church. Extra weapons were distributed. Lofty and I, the 'long' and the 'short' of the Troop, were assigned to a two-inch mortar team under the command of Hoggy, the troop sergeant. Oxy was given the mortar to carry; Lofty and I were each to carry two cases of bombs making 36 in all.

The assault began. Rushing from the house, we dropped down under cover of the nearer wall of the road as intermittent machine-gun fire raked the road. By a break in the wall, we waited the order to dash across the road, one by one, to a gap in the further wall. As I awaited my turn to cross, I had just time for a gloomy reflection on the possibility of a bullet hitting my cases of mortar bombs. When my time came, I made my dash and arrived safely across. Lofty followed unscathed. Everyone seemed to have made the crossing without injury until it was found that Dinty had been wounded in the hand. We left him behind to await aid while our dash up the hillside continued. We in the mortar team took up a position behind the church and, soon, Hoggy and Oxy had the mortar in action. We heard the first three bombs explode but then we were puzzled that, after firing more bombs, no further explosions were heard. Soon, we realized that, in the excitement of the moment, the caps on each bomb had not been removed. The first three bombs had exploded only because of hitting the hard pantiles on the roof of the enemy held farmhouse. Lofty and I began, speedily, to remove the caps while Oxy fired away.

Meanwhile, Johnny, the squadron commander, had climbed into the tower of the church and was observing the enemy held farmhouse and our own mortar fire. Then we heard his call to Hoggy, 'Sergeant Hodgkinson! Right 50!'

Lofty, whose name was Wright but, because of a number of Wrights in the Squadron, was known as Wright 50, the last two digits of his army number making the distinction, suddenly sprang to his full height and shouted, 'Here, Sir!'

At that very moment, a burst of machine-gun fire clipped leaves and branches of a tree above his head. His return to the prone position exceeded all records in speed.

With all our mortar bombs fired, Hoggy ordered me to dash back for more. I did not relish the danger of crossing the road again and when I saw a supporting troop about to climb the hill, I relieved the mortar-bomb carrier of his load saying that they were needed urgently. I rushed back up the hill to surprise Hoggy with the speed of my return.

Then, as the mortar began to fire again, from the crypt of the church came whiffs of a most appetizing, mouth-watering smell of cooked beef. Two or three riflemen went down the outside steps to investigate. Imagine our surprise when they emerged guarding two shocked soldiers of the German 4th Parachute Division. They had been blissfully unaware of the battle above and were frying beef for their comrades who, little did they know, had beat a hasty retreat.

As the afternoon wore on, so the first heavy rain of autumn began to fall, soaking through our thin khaki drill uniforms. Lofty and I sought shelter by burrowing into some stooks of corn which were scattered about. Then, orders were given that we were to hold on to our gains and 16 Troop moved into the nave of the church. Cockney George, whose ingenuity knew no bounds, shed his dripping wet clothing. Then, regardless both of his being a Roman Catholic and of the sanctity of the altar cloth, wrapped his near-naked body in its warm, dry folds.

As night fell, fears of an enemy counter-attack rose. Lofty and I, cold and uncomfortable in our sodden clothing, were posted, with a Bren gun, in the loft of a nearby barn. For the rest of the night we lay catnapping at times but mostly peering with tense expectancy, through an unglazed window, into the enveloping darkness. Fortunately, there was no response from the enemy and with daylight came the unexpected order to withdraw. Our advance had taken us over a mile beyond the 6th Gordons, the most forward battalion of the 2nd Infantry Brigade. It was deemed that

C Squadron was too isolated and we withdrew to our original start line. Few of us relished the thought of having to retake the church.

Sixteen Troop occupied a farmhouse. In the cellar below, fearful of shelling and the likelihood of battle, an extended Italian family had crowded. From a bedroom, which became an observation post, we kept watch over the rising ground before us. Between our watches, we used a convenient double bed in an adjoining bedroom for rest and much-needed sleep. On my coming off duty, I was surprised to find that a wizened, old Italian woman, unable to endure the squalid and crowded conditions in the cellar, lay fully clothed and slantwise on the bed, in a deep sleep of exhaustion. I had not the heart to waken her so I pushed her to one side and lay down unwilling to lose the chance of sleep.

On the following day, we began a patrol to make contact with an enemy which we believed was slowly disengaging and retiring towards the Gothic Line, a strong defence line, some distance to the north.

We set off in Indian file. I was operating my number 38 wireless set, a small and light 'transceiver' with a throat microphone. We had not been on our way long when we were met by a short, scruffy civilian carrying a large wicker basket full of grapes and peaches. These he offered as an excuse to accompany the patrol in order to seek his daughter who, he said, had been taken away by the Germans.

For a while, he trailed behind us until we approached a hillside village. Our commander would have him come no further, whereupon he sat down glumly against a stone wall. Under cover of the wall, we approached the village. The warning signs were there. A foreboding, unnatural silence persisted. No dogs barked to signal our presence. We knew that the inhabitants would be below ground in the safety of their cellars. Two of the patrol went forward and entered the nearest house. It was unoccupied but there was evidence that it was being used by the enemy. On a table, they found an alarm clock with a setting of 4 a.m. A casual glance through a rear window brought surprise and alarm for the two men. From the woods behind and above the village, they saw several enemy soldiers emerge and descend towards them. Taking the alarm clock with them, the two dashed back to where we lay waiting. I reported the news over the air and Johnny ordered our patrol to return. As we withdrew under the cover of the long wall, we found that the Italian and his fruit had disappeared.

We returned to the farmhouse to be told that, on the next day, we would be probing deeper into the territory to our front. To sustain us in our task, we were to carry our own food in the form of tins of stew borne in hessian bags. We would have to share these cumbersome, extra burdens as we proceeded.

An altogether different greeting awaited us as we approached the village which was the objective of the previous day's patrol. The villagers were out in force to line the uneven, cobbled thoroughfare. They clapped, slapped our backs and cheered as we passed through. On we went by hill and through valley, on through woodland where we found signs of a hurried enemy withdrawal. Small wooden signposts in German marked the former locations of army units. But of the enemy there was no sign.

By evening, wetted by heavy, intermittent rain and weary after our long tramp, we stopped at an isolated house. Feeling 'down in the dumps', tired and exhausted, we entered. Under the cloud of our low spirits, we threw caution to the winds, made a roaring fire in a grate and steam dried our clinging, wet battle dress as we sat. Then a very minimum of guards were posted as snatches of sleep were taken by those off duty.

By morning, we were in a different frame of mind and, before we set off on patrol, two decisions were made. The first was to jettison some of the weighty tins of stew and the second, by way of thanks for the night's shelter, to secretly stuff the surplus tins of stew into the drawers of a sideboard to benefit the hungry family who lived in the house.

Another day of trying to make contact began. By noon, we had reached a smallholding with a small vineyard alongside. The grapes were ready for gathering and hung in large bunches. Our thirst was great and so was the temptation to slake it. Dinky and I, unable to resist, were about to walk between two rows of vines when, suddenly, from a small window, high up in the gable of the house, a woman's voice shrieked, 'Niente! Niente!'

In whatever language 'no' has the ring of authority and we stopped short. Our lives were most probably saved by her intervention for, between the rows, there were sown several German

Schu (S) mines, those most devastating anti-personnel contrivances.

To our front, about a mile further on up the widening valley, we could see a collection of houses which may have been on the periphery of the town of Leccio. As we could see no movement in that direction, Foxy and a trooper commandeered two cycles and rode along the road towards the houses. Almost immediately, their presence was greeted by a salvo of mortar bombs exploding close by them. Hurriedly dismounting they left the road and dived for cover. They arrived back safely, without their cycles but none the worse for their ordeal.

Now, for the first time in two days of patrolling and in an advance of twelve miles, we had encountered the enemy. I sent the news of our making contact, In turn, squadron headquarters informed us that our mission was over. The 2nd American Corps, on our left, was about to take over the 1st Divisional Sector.

We began to plod back and after four miles we met the leading troops of an American Regimental Combat Team which was resting at the side of a track. There, in their combat boots, they looked more footsore than we did. As we passed by, the GIs asked the same pertinent question: 'How far ahead is the Kraut?'

Making light of the answer, we were able to say that they would have to travel a few more miles before meeting up with Jerry.

We returned to Florence where regimental headquarters was established in a tobacco factory. There we awaited orders to enter the front line again. Meanwhile, the 3rd Brigade was advancing in hill country beyond Florence and to the west of Borgo San Lorenzo. By 11 September 1944, the regiment had begun its own operations on the right flank of 3rd Brigade. Patrolling was active and vigorous in order to keep in contact with the German forces, now withdrawing into their main defences of the Gothic Line. There, the Apennines rose steeply. Half the way up the steep slopes, the enemy had built bunkers, laid land mines and had erected barbed wire entanglements. Few tracks and footpaths led upwards and the only important road north was the one defined as 'Arrow Route'. It was a tortuous, winding way which, in places, was carved into the hillsides.

While 3rd Brigade's advance was astride 'Arrow Route', the Regiment began its probing of the Gothic Line defences. Patrols found the enemy in position near to a railway tunnel close to La

Tomba and north of the village of Gattaia. By 14 September, troop positions had been established to the north-east of Vezzano, from which further patrols went forward. They found that the Germans had abandoned their positions around La Tomba and the railway tunnel. Indeed, all along the divisional front, pressure was beginning to tell. With the capture of Prefetto by the 66th Infantry Brigade and with the advance of our own regiment, breaches in the Gothic Line had been made. With these successes, the 1st British Infantry Division became the first formation of 13th Corps to break through.

In foul weather, through the muddy and difficult mountainous terrain, the infantry battalions continued their forward thrust astride of 'Arrow Route'. To support their efforts, both Indian mule teams and Italian pack-horse teams were summoned to bring up supplies and return the wounded on panniers. Such were the circumstances that there was no immediate role for the 1st Reconnaissance Regiment in the hills and it was withdrawn to its rest area close to Borgo San Lorenzo. It was there that Paddy attended a conference of commanding officers. It was suggested that his soldiers might be used in the hilly terrain to carry up ammunition, on foot, for the field guns which were supporting the forward battalions. He was infuriated by the suggestion and replied that his men were combat troops and he would rather they remain so.

Paddy's insistence brought a quick end to our stay in the rest area. The regiment was seconded to a composite force under the command of 26th Armoured Brigade Group. In the now accepted custom of reverting to an infantry role, the regiment was taken in trucks eastward to Portico, from where C Squadron was sent forward to San Benedetto in Alpi, a small mountain village.

There, 16 Troop prepared for a further advance, by night, to seize and hold a farmhouse on the road from San Benedetto to Rocca San Casciano.

For my part, I was equipped with both a field telephone and a drum of cable wire which I unrolled along the edge of the road as we proceeded. Soon, we encountered two deep, wide holes in the road. Following behind the others, I skirted the demolitions with my cable.

As we approached warily, the farmhouse loomed closer. The

troop stopped to listen for tell-tale sounds and movement. Nothing stirred. Tensely, and quickly, we moved forward to find the farm and outbuildings unoccupied. But, inside, in a bare bedroom where I was to set up the field telephone, there was evidence of recent enemy usage. In a corner, there were one or two loaves of black bread. More than that, my sensitive nose had picked up the faint scent of talc which, from past experience, I associated with German officers.

First, I began to black out the single window, to enable me to use the troop commander's torch and so set up my field telephone. As I was trying to fasten up a sheet against the window, I heard one burst of fire from a sub-machine-gun, which was followed immediately by explosions on the wall of the house. Two German stick-grenades had been thrown. From some distance away, there followed prolonged bursts of Spandau machine-gun fire which spattered and sprayed against the wall. With no mean haste, I dropped flat below the window and lay, thankfully unhurt, until, at length, the firing stopped and I was able to finish the blacking-out of the window.

A minute or two later, from out of the darkness, they brought in the gentle Young Harry and laid him on the floor. He was able to say that, while he was at his post, close to the road, he saw two figures emerge above the banked further side of the road. He challenged them only to receive, at close range, one burst from a Schmeisser light machine-gun.

By the light of the torch, we found his injuries. There were several small calibre bullet wounds puncturing his arm and his ribcage. He needed aid as quickly as possible. Again, there was neither stretcher nor stretcher bearers. Again, we improvised. With rope, barrel to barrel, we lashed two rifles together. By the same method, we lashed together two more, making the carrying poles. A search of the house yielded a strip of carpet which we pierced with holes down each long side, threading rope through the holes and round the rifles. We had created a crude stretcher.

Four of the tallest and strongest of the troop – Dobbsy, Col, Jimmy and Glyn – were given the back-breaking task of carrying Young Harry back to the nearest aid post but, when we gently lowered our comrade on to the stretcher, we found, to our distress, that the carpet was too short and that the poor lad would have to be carried with his legs dangling. Manfully, the four set off on an almost intolerable journey. They toiled with great difficulty, particularly when they reached the road demolitions. At last, they found help. Young Harry had borne his pain without complaint. With speed, he was rushed to a field hospital. But it seemed that great endeavour by his four comrades was in vain. The outcome was one of sadness for 16 Troop. Under surgery for a ruptured spleen, the gentle Young Harry died of his wounds.

After our efforts in getting Young Harry away and having set up the field telephone, I tried to call squadron headquarters. The line was dead. Out of contact, 16 Troop spent a wretched night of frequent alarms and 'stands to arms', always in fear of an enemy attack in strength. In between our manning of hastily dug slit trenches, we took turns to rest on the bare floor of the bedroom, our weapons at the ready. Oxy and I, having finished our watch, lay side by side. Carelessly, I took off my spectacles and placed them nearby. Inevitably, there came the call to 'stand to'. Oxy, in his haste, unwittingly stood on my spectacles and shattered the lenses. My spare pair had been left back at squadron headquarters. Now, I was purblind and faced the prospect of a new day with trepidation.

On the following morning, Sherman tanks of the 17th/21st Lancers roared up from behind. Having passed our positions, they debouched on to adjoining land to begin a determined sortie into enemy lines. It was while they were hotly engaging the enemy, that two of us took the chance to walk back in search of the fault on the telephone cable. We followed the line back along the side of the road until we came across the reason for the fault. Close to the road demolitions, a part of the cable had been chopped into several pieces by vehicles or tanks attempting, by night, to get round the craters in the road. Having found the two ends of the wire, we were able to carry out repairs. As we returned, the Lancers were still in action but, just as we reached our forward position the tanks were beginning to return.

We looked with envy at the first tank to pass. It was turretless, being especially designed to carry wounded. Two casualties lay on stretchers which were anchored on either side of a large cavity over which the turret would have been mounted. The wounded were receiving aid as the tank moved back. In my thoughts was the supposition that Young Harry may have survived through such immediate aid and quick evacuation to hospital.

After the tanks had gone, 16 Troop was ordered to move forward and occupy another farm closer to Rocca San Casciano. Again I carried the field telephone and reeled out the cable. Although the loss of good vision was a handicap, communication with squadron headquarters had to be maintained. Without retaliation by the enemy, 16 Troop occupied the farm. Communication was established. But, no sooner were we settled than the shelling began. What is more, we realized, with consternation and dismay, that the shells were coming from behind, from our own guns.

In a ground-floor room, we took immediate action, manhandling huge, heavy sacks of grain and jamming them into the window space for protection. Then, crouching under a heavy, wooden table with the troop commander, with great concern and urgency in my voice, I called by phone for a quick end to the shelling. Soon, to our relief, the guns ceased firing. It was not until some time later that we were informed that the bombardment came from a battery of medium howitzers, firing heavy 5.5-inch shells. We were thankful that the guns had not caused casualties.

As night fell, we were ordered into Rocca San Casciano and set up troop headquarters in a large house which we were told had been abandoned by a fleeing, wealthy fascist. The house came under fire from a solitary German self-propelled gun which fired heavy calibre shells into the town. Being on watch outside of the house was a frightening experience; there was time only to drop flat and rely on good fortune, for the muffled sound of the gun and the crash of the shell were almost simultaneous.

Early the next day, 14 Troop took up the lead and moved on to the hillside beyond the town. From a farm, a few hundred yards above, the leading patrol received a burst of Spandau machine-gun fire. The leading scout was wounded. Two of the patrol crawled forward to his aid, only to be pinned down by further bursts of fire. A calculated risk had to be taken. 'Cotty', the squadron first aid corporal, and another man put Red Cross bands on their arms and boldly went forward. Without coming under fire, they were able to carry the casualty away without harm. Throughout our campaigning, this was the second gesture of compassion by German troops for the wounded and respect for the Geneva Convention that we had encountered.

Fourteen Troop, held up in their advance by the enemy's machine-gun which was dominating the lower slopes, awaited support from the artillery; but help came in a different way. C Squadron received the news that relief by the 2nd Polish Corps was imminent. In anticipation, we awaited its coming. Soon, the town began to fill with General Ander's tough combat troops, speaking a guttural, Germanic language which we could not understand.

We left them to continue where we had left off and C Squadron moved back to Borgo San Lorenzo. There, with little time to rest and recover, we heard that we were about to be committed to battle again. This time we were not only to be facing a stubborn, German defence line but also we were to fight against a morale-sapping, bitter winter in the high Apennines.

Thirteen

Mountain Warfare

Along the whole length of its front line, the American 5th Army was at a standstill. Having played its part in the destruction of the Gothic Line, its divisions, like those of the 13th British Corps, had battled relentlessly forward through formidable mountainous terrain, in worsening weather and along rapidly deteriorating supply routes. There was a shortage of ammunition and an increasing exhaustion of its combat troops. Relief became a necessity.

Subsequently, a realignment of the front line was ordered. Thirteenth Corps of the British 8th Army was asked to extend to its left, to take over the critical Monte Grande sector, a sensitive salient bulging into the enemy defences before Bologna. In accordance, 1st British Infantry Division was ordered to relieve the 88th United States (General Custer) Division, even though the British had been in the front line longer than their counterparts. Since its breaching of the Gothic Line, its infantry battalions had fought their way forward with great determination and gallantry. In atrocious weather, they had overcome several stubborn mountain strongholds of the enemy. On Monte Ceco, after making several unsuccessful attempts to gain the summit, it was left to the Dukes (The Duke of Wellington's Regiment) to take the mountaintop by storm. Great sadness and high honour were the outcome. Lieutenant Colonel Shiel, the Duke's Commander, was killed by shell fire during the attack: 5891907, Private R Burton, was awarded the Victoria Cross for valour in the same action.

Now, both for 1st Infantry Division in general and for 1st Reconnaissance Regiment in particular, further mountain warfare was to be their lot. The regiment was again to take its part alongside the infantry battalions in terrain where only foot soldiers and mules could go and where rain, mist wind and snow were to be cruel and undesirable bedfellows.

The prospect was daunting. Between 1st Division's rest area at Borgo San Lorenzo and the front line lay forty miles of inhospitable mountain territory. There were no forward assembly areas. The roads leading to the Monte Grande sector were so bad that they became inaccessible to nearly all vehicles except those with four-wheel drive. Troops had to be taken forward and backward in four-wheel drive GMC covered wagons driven by Americans. Rest periods were short and curtailed on account of travelling time to the front and back again.

On top of these restrictions was the news that the numbers of men manning the front line would be less than those of the Americans being relieved. The 1st Division would relieve the equivalent of eleven battalions with only seven battalions of its own infantry. A further worrying prospect was that because of the Second Front and, consequently, the drying up of reinforcements from England, each infantry battalion would be reduced to three rifle companies instead of four.

For 1st Division, the commitment, before relief, was expected to last six weeks. In the event, it lasted for nearly three months in the dead of winter.

By 11 November 1944, C Squadron was ready to enter the front line. Its orders were to relieve B Squadron which was already holding the San Clemente road block, in the Sillaro valley, on the right flank of the Monte Grande sector.

Heavily loaded with equipment and weaponry, we scrambled aboard the awaiting American six-wheeled trucks to begin the journey through the mountains. After several hours' drive on bumpy, imperfect roads, heavy with military traffic, the trucks arrived in an open area about a mile behind the San Clemente road block.

Here, the Sillaro valley bottom had widened considerably; so much so that it had become a staging area and a suitable space for supporting arms. On its forward edge, one of our field regiments of 25-pounder guns was in action. To the right, where the valley was flat, several Sherman tanks of the 11th Canadian Armoured

Regiment were in place, ready to fire indirectly if needed. Their crews were dug in cosily under their tanks.

We were soon to envy them for, as we alighted from the trucks, from the enemy came the first ranging shells, bursting overhead in black, menacing puffs of smoke, the heralds of high explosive shells to come. As they began to whine and explode, we dived for the only doubtful protection beneath the trucks. We hugged the earth, held our breath and hoped. Alongside of me, in the dark, below the chassis, I saw clearly the whites of the Black driver's eyes. If they were manifesting fear, then mine must have been whiter.

At last the shelling ceased and we emerged unscathed. With great haste, we assembled in sections and marched forward in single file along the muddy, crumbling road. As night fell, we began our relief of B Squadron. Its troopers gave us this advice: 'Keep your heads down, make no obvious movement or noise and you may avoid unpleasant attention from Jerry.'

We discovered that our positions were grouped around farm buildings, several of which had been demolished by enemy shelling. Underneath the ruins, rest places had been made simply by burrowing into and beneath the debris.

In the small stock yard, we were surprised to find a solitary Sherman tank which had been left unmanned since the Americans left. It remained so until a crew of the 11th Canadian Armoured Regiment came from behind to take possession.

It was our good fortune that they came, for a stray cow had wandered into the front line. It had been hit by shrapnel and lowed incessantly and pitifully. We contemplated dispatching it with a single shot but we were spared this action by two of the Canadian tank crew. They had been slaughterers in civilian life so, without compunction, they roped the suffering beast, dragged it to a barn, hoisted it on a beam and ended its misery with a revolver shot. Then they produced knives and began the removal of the hide and the preparation of the carcass. Their intention was to provide fresh beef for their own unit as well as for other units in the area.

For six days, the squadron held the San Clemente road block quietly, as recommended by B Squadron. In that time, again, I was attached to 17 Troop and joined Jack's section. Since my last attachment there had been hardly any change. The enduring bosom pals, Buck and Waterhouse, were still together, my Anzio comrade, Albie, and 'Parksie', a lance-corporal, made up the section.

We were required to go out on an ambush patrol. Our task was to prepare an ambush round a bridge, over the Sillaro river, some 600 yards beyond our positions. Parksie, newly promoted and experiencing leadership for the first time, led us under cover of a wall, towards the bridge. Having got there, he posted us round the bridge. Tensely and silently, we watched and waited throughout the long hours of the night. We waited in vain. No enemy patrol ventured our way. At last, just before dawn, stiffly and wearily, we began to move back, wet from frequent rain showers and exhausted with strain.

When we were half of the way back, suddenly it was light; Parksie had miscalculated the time. We were in full view of enemy observation posts. With ears cocked I listened intently for familiar sounds. They came; the muffled thump of mortars firing. Instantaneously, I tapped Parksie's shoulder with my Bren gun and dropped flat into a shallow man-made drainage channel beneath the wall at the side of the road, one which I had noticed when we were on our way to the bridge. Parksie reacted instantly as did the rest of the patrol behind me. At the same time, mortar bombs began to explode both on and near to the road. Those that hit the road sent a hail of shrapnel against the stone wall. The shallow channel beneath the wall, only one foot deep, had given us just enough protection. We rose shaken but unharmed and quickly moved along the line of the wall until we reached our own positions.

Our commitment in the San Clemente valley came to an end on 22 November 1944. A further alignment of the front line was ordered. The 78th (Battleaxe) Division, on our right flank, began to extend to the left to take over a part of the 1st British Infantry Division's scantily held Monte Grande sector. We were told that the London Irish Rifles of the Irish Brigade would relieve C Squadron at ten in the evening. By midnight, we were to take up new front line positions on the extreme left flank of the sector.

As we prepared to march out at the appointed hour, we heard, with dismay and misgivings, the noise of vehicles' engines, occasional shouts and the clanking of arms. Ruefully, we thought that the London Irish were making too much of a 'song and dance' as a prelude to their taking over. The Germans thought so too and began their own 'concerto': a heavy shelling of the area. Our departure was delayed as we took cover to await the end of the barrage. Then, we marched out as quickly as we could in an endeavour to make up for lost time. From the Sillaro valley, two more valleys branched at right angles into the Monte Grande sector. The Americans had named them the Boston Byway and the Western Valley. We took the former route and, in the darkness, climbed laboriously upwards to the ridge of the Rignano Spur which separated the two valleys. In full equipment, the going was hard and exhausting so that, by the time we had reached Monte Cuccoli, it was near to dawn, allowing us little time to join A Squadron on Marzolina.

Marzolina was a bare, treeless ridge stretching parallel to the enemy positions, which were on the facing slopes across a valley. Atop Marzolina was a solitary, shell-damaged, one-storey building which was abandoned and used only as a shelter at night. On the forward slopes of the ridge, defensive strong points had been built, and further forward slit trenches had been dug and used as observation posts during daylight. On the reverse slopes, squadron headquarters and day rest positions had been dug into the hillside. Further down the slope still and only 400 yards behind the front line, in a small group of farm buildings, Paddy had set up his regimental headquarters. To the left and right, he had deployed his mortar troop which, with its close support weapons, was invaluable.

Paddy, confident of his soldiers' ability and infantry experience, had informed the divisional commander that he was prepared to commit his regiment to the holding of Marzolina Ridge permanently, and that he would find his own reliefs as well as forming an unchanging link with the 85th American Division on the left of 1st Division.

So, the plan for the winter was carried out. Always there would be two squadrons holding the front line while one squadron rested in the divisional rear area around Borgo San Lorenzo. The days of rest, in reality, were only three because two were taken up by travelling to, and preparing for another spell on, Marzolina.

As we began our rounds of front-line duties and rest periods, the days grew shorter, the cold strengthened and the weather worsened. We were really not equipped to stand the new conditions. Before any windproof or winter clothing arrived to give extra protection, we made do with a batch of Royal Engineers' leather jerkins. But it was our feet which suffered the most. Our leather boots were never dry. Damp and cold penetrated to the bone and we had cause to envy our adversaries in their jackboots. We reverted to wrapping our boots and calves in empty hessian sand bags but they did little to ease our discomfort.

By day, we slept fitfully in the knowledge that often and without warning, the mountain mists would fall, under cover of which we would dash forward to man the advanced positions. But it was by night that we were most active. Frequent patrols of all kinds were mounted. On Paddy's insistence, we had to dominate the valley between ourselves and the enemy.

On one such patrol, unwittingly, I became the central figure in an incident that would have been considered hilarious if it had not been so serious. I was Bren gunner in Jack's section. He had been ordered to take out his patrol with the objective of keeping watch on a house on the lower slopes of the enemy's positions. There we were to ascertain whether the Germans were using the house by night. The patrol was to go out twice during the night, each time keeping a two-hour vigil.

As Bren gunner, I was allowed, at least for the first stages, to carry the machine-gun on my shoulder rather than in the tiring 'trail arms' position. Jack led the way out, followed by myself, Buck, Waterhouse and Albie. We plodded down a track, ankle deep in mud. In our boots, heavily plastered in mud, we squelched and slid our way down towards the objective. Soon, Jack gave the signal to drop to the ground. As I lowered my Bren gun, to my horror, I saw that it had no barrel. I whispered the shocking news to Jack. Oblivious of our nearness to the enemy, he replied with a much too loud string of oaths, made the worse by my remark that now, all I could do was to throw the thing at the enemy.

Having exhausted his tirade, Jack ordered us to crawl nearer to the house. In slimy mud which coated our greatcoats, our trousered knees and our elbows, we felt like snails as we left smooth, muddy trails shining in the moonlight. Ahead, we could see the house more clearly against the darker backdrop of the slope. We stopped, watched and waited as the dampness seeped through our clothing. Miserable and disarmed, I lay with my barrel-less gun pointing uselessly towards the house.

Then, the long, tense, two hours ended. The house remained silent and still. Jack led us back up the same muddy track into our positions. Half way back, to my surprise and relief, I came across the gun barrel, sticking upright in the mud. I could think only that the barrel locking nut had caught in my webbing shoulder straps and loosened so that the barrel had dropped into the mud without a sound.

Having arrived back, and in the confines of a slit trench and hampered by the darkness, I did my best to clean both the barrel and the gun. Before long, we sallied forth again for our next two hours' watch over the house. Again, we waited silent and watchful until Jack seemed to have had enough. He believed that he had seen the flare of a lighted match within the house. With my reconstituted Bren gun, he ordered me to crawl forward to a small knoll from where I was to fire off a magazine after he had opened fire with his tommy-gun. As the heavy calibre bullets sped overhead, I pressed the trigger of my Bren gun. Nothing happened. I carried out the immediate action of re-cocking and pressing the trigger. Again the gun failed to fire. Helpless, I waited anxiously until I was sure that Jack had expended his ammunition. Then I crawled back and whispered, sheepishly, that my gun wouldn't fire. After another flow of invectives condemning my uselessness, we began the second leg-wearying climb back. The 'Comedy Of Errors' was over. Thankfully, the German parachute troops did not get in on the act.

After sixteen days in the line and five days' rest, C Squadron returned to Marzolina. This time, from the Sillaro Valley, our route upwards was through the Western Valley. As we entered, by sections, in single file, we passed a battery of 25-pounders, its guns emplaced in firing positions we had not seen before. With their trails dug into the ground and their wheels elevated on ammunition boxes, the guns were firing in what the artillery men called the Upper Register. This ploy enabled them to gain a high trajectory in order to clear the ridges and so give closer support to the forward troops.

The scene in the valley needs further description. A stream flowed from side to side on a meandering course until it reached the larger Sillaro river. In turn, it was fed by smaller streamlets flowing from the spurs on either side. Consequently, the valley bottom appeared to be a sea of waterlogged mud. American and British engineers, in turn, had laid a track into the valley and had built several trestle bridges over traversing streams.

Further up the valley, we arrived at the Jeep-head, the furthest point beyond which no vehicle could pass. It was the starting point for the mule-transport companies before they began their steep climb with ammunition and supplies.

Here, there was deep, clinging, glutinous mud, made worse by the sinking hooves of mules and the passage of men. With their heads drooping in the rain, the waiting mules stood looking bedraggled and miserable, their Indian muleteers standing or squatting in their protective capes as the beating rain added to their discomfort.

Here, too, on the muddy lower slopes above the Jeep-head, in the all embracing mud was 'Butlin's Holiday Camp', a collection of dug-in lean-tos and bivouac covered slit trenches, where the reserve counter-attack battalion of the northern sector existed. At this time, the holiday-makers were the 1st Battalion, the Loyal Regiment.

Now, we began our long climb upwards on what the Americans had colourfully named 'Sunset Trail'. Almost at once, the Trail rose steeply. The gradient was such that the engineers of the 23rd Field Company were constructing an artificial stair of lengths of chestnut paling which served as steps and enabled both us and the mules to get a grip on the slippery slope.

Suddenly, I was surprised to hear my name being called by one of the engineers. It came from a man called Nobby who had been my Sunday School teacher in the not too distant past. A few precious moments of greeting was all I was allowed before we were climbing upwards again. We followed the line of a ridge, sloping steeply on either side. Here we trod carefully, for a slip and a roll down would have meant an exhausting climb back. From time to time, we came across stiffened carcasses of dead mules, the legacies of earlier enemy shelling.

When, at last, we reached the Marzolina slit trenches, we were greeted by an enemy mortar barrage. (Nobby, the engineer, told me that when he heard the barrage, he said a prayer for my safety.) After the hostile welcome, C Squadron settled down to its tour of duty. The manning of the forward positions was left mainly to the scout troops. Night patrolling was undertaken on the whole by 17 Troop, to which again I was attached.

A cycle of four nights was devised. For three nights in four, various kinds of patrols went out. On the fourth night, instead of patrolling, 17 Troop became the counter-attack force. In a ruined building, between the floor joists, the men rested. Sleep came in short snatches for it was bitterly cold and, in full equipment, we were uncomfortable. With our weapons at the ready, we awaited the alarm which, if given, would send us rushing forward to regain lost ground.

Because of 17 Troop's continuous night work, with its subsequent tension and fatigue, Paddy's thoughtful tactic was to withdraw us for rest by day to a barn close to his regimental headquarters. So, each day, we rested, fed and slept until night fell and patrolling began. Often, rain and occasional sleet were the enemies. Apart from an odd skirmish and a trickle of casualties, sickness and exhaustion were the more likely to reduce the ranks.

On 21 December 1944, C Squadron was relieved and pleased to have the good fortune of being able to spend Christmas in the rest area. Then, the blow fell for two sections of 17 Troop. They were to remain behind for another two days, to perform a new and laborious task, that of repairing roads. The road through the Sillaro valley, being under heavy and continuous use, was crumbling in parts. Engineers were striving to shore up and rebuild the damaged sections.

Of course Jack's section was one of the two chosen, so, in the twilight, we pitched two-man bivouacs where we could find a ledge of level ground on the slopes above the valley bottom. Rain was falling heavily and streamlets of muddy water began to flow down the slopes, threatening to wash us out of our tents. We spent a miserable night crouched and sleepless under the canvas as the liquid mud seeped underneath and into the bivouac.

On the following morning, we began our work with the engineers some of whom, in wellington boots, waded into the shallow parts of the Sillaro river towards huge, fallen boulders. When one was found of suitable size, they attached an explosive device called a 'Bee Hive' in order to shatter a boulder into manageable pieces. Our job was to paddle in our already soaked boots, collect the fragmented stones and load them into the bucket of a bulldozer waiting on the bank. We followed the loaded vehicle until it reached the point where the road was being repaired. There, a drainage ditch had been dug and the road had been shored up with stakes. We threw the small boulders into a gap behind the stakes, building up a hard core of stone to the depth of about two feet.

Backwards and forwards we laboured, driving our already wearied bodies to the limit. From time to time, we took rests and perceived how important was the task to keep open this vital road. Constantly, vehicles carrying front-line troops, supplies and ammunition passed by. At intervals, back from the front, came the inevitable casualties. They were being carried in ambulances of the American field service driven by their splendid, volunteer drivers; men who had failed their medical examination for service in the United States armed forces but who were now driving their four-wheeled drive ambulances where our own could not go. Through clear windows, we saw wounded comrades receiving blood transfusions. 'Poor b—g—rs,' we muttered as, inspired, we began to work with greater zeal and effort.

With the task completed, on the night of 23 December a truck came to take us back to Borgo San Lorenzo. That evening, the snow began to fall and the cold was intense. We sat in the back of the truck hunched and huddled together, trying to gain some warmth from the closeness of our bodies.

It was a nightmare of a journey back not only because of the raging blizzard but also because we were not out of range of enemy shelling. In Castel Del Rio, we were stopped by a military policeman and told that a heavy gun was shelling the streets and that the driver ought to drive 'hell for leather' out of the town.

Our route back was long and arduous and it was not until first light on Christmas Eve that we arrived, chilled and stiff, in the rest area. As I rejoined 16 Troop, its men were just rising from their makeshift beds on the floor of a barn. Dinky, of the Bicycle Club, seeing my condition, encouraged me to undress and get straight into the bed he had just left. Between the blankets it was unbelievably warm and I fell at once into a deep and dreamless sleep.

By Christmas Day, I had recovered enough to think of Christmas dinner which had been contrived with difficulty by Corporal Bill and his helpers. In a wooden, ramshackle hut which served as the local village hall, we sat down to a hot meal with unexpected turkey on the menu. Two turkeys had been provided from a source other than that of the Quartermaster. They had been purloined by the men of 16 Troop in the mistaken belief that the Italians with whom they shared the farm building had stolen all the spare boots left behind while the Troop was in the front line.

For the men harbouring this belief, the two turkeys were fair game for a reprisal. When the birds wandered out of the safety of the farmyard, they were waylaid and, without ceremony, lost their heads with two strokes of a bayonet.

Now it was Dobbsy's turn to act. He took it upon himself to dress the turkeys. He spent an uncomfortable hour in a feather spitting task inside a tarpaulin-covered Bren carrier. By the light of a vehicle inspection lamp, he managed to prepare the birds for the table. Later, much to everyone's regret, it was discovered that the boot-stealing marauders had been men of a nearby regiment.

The Christmas meal was washed down with generous quantities of the notorious 'Stella' beer and the even more notorious 'Red Biddy': a cheap, potent, Italian red wine. As the beer and wine was imbibed so spirits rose and foolhardiness grew. Relief from tense and wearing front-line duties manifested itself in improprieties. Later, we lined up in the hope of a Christmas tea, but it was nonexistent (the cooks being the worse for drink). We were, however, entertained by the spectacle of Kench, the squadron sergeant-major, and Syd, the squadron storeman, both of whom, after a bout of drinking, had begun a bout of fisticuffs, blissfully unaware of the cheering spectators.

More was to follow later. Some inebriated men of 17 Troop, wandering about in their merry perambulations, found Kench, heavily sleeping off the effects of both drink and exertion. Their daring knew no bounds for, as he lay in his misappropriated caravan, they hitched it to a 15 cwt truck and towed the oblivious Kench and his caravan into the wilds of the countryside. A search party was mustered to find Kench who, to his credit, took no action against the culprits. Who could condemn them for their prank? They had endured weeks in the front line, in appalling weather, and soon they would be back for another round of duty.

On 28 December 1944, C Squadron, less the two sections of 17 Troop, relieved A Squadron. Following their work with the engineers, two Sections were to follow two days later. But, for me, it was not to be. I was ordered to rejoin 16 Troop. I was aggrieved by the decision to curtail my rest period and went to argue my case with 'Trots', a lieutenant on duty in the rest area. He told me that Arty, a fellow trooper, had reported sick with back trouble and, consequently, he was adamant that I would have to go. I joined 16 Troop for the journey to the front.

Later, after Jack's section had rejoined 17 Troop, I was seconded again, both to his section and to share in wireless duties. Soon, Albie and I found ourselves in an all-night standing patrol. He was armed with a rifle, I with a newfangled weapon called a PIAT (Projectile Infantry Anti-Tank). It seemed to be an outlandish weapon. It was hard to cock and load its projectile which resembled a large spinning top, with a thin point of hardened steel. No vehicles, let alone tanks, had managed to scale the heights of our mountain bastion and when I questioned the weapon's use, I was told to fire on approaching enemy foot patrols.

On a night of biting cold, we crouched in our outpost slit trench, our booted feet and legs swathed in empty hessian sandbags, our unrolled gas capes spread over our great-coated bodies in order to keep in some body heat. The night was enlivened by bursts of machine-gun fire from both sides. From the German side, firing on fixed lines, a Spandau, with sewing-machine rapidity, was raking the Marzolina ridge high above and well behind us. In reply, from the ridge, a Vickers Medium machine-gun, with a steady and circumspect beat, discharged streams of bullets into the enemy held hills. Well beneath the trajectory, we were more concerned with keeping warm.

At midnight, we were visited by 'Tight So', a young lieutenant. From a bottle, he offered us a ration of rum which we declined, being unwilling to concede the degree of warmth we had engendered beneath the canopy of our gas capes.

Tight So left us to make his way upwards to the troop positions, higher up the slope. There, he must have had more than his fair share of the rum ration, for this appeared to have clouded his judgement. When Paddy called on the field telephone to order him to get a bearing on the troublesome Spandau, he sent back a map reference which sited the machine gun in the Mediterranean Sea between Corsica and the Italian mainland. Paddy was incensed and informed Tight So that he would give him fifteen minutes to get an accurate bearing on the gun or that he would have his commission taken from him.

This threat must have induced an immediate sobriety, for a new and more accurate reference was forthcoming. Evidently, with his anger allayed, Paddy had relented and took no further action against the offender.

A few days later, it was Albie and I who were assigned to a day observation post which we manned before dawn and left after nightfall. The observation post was a glorified slit trench, larger than normal and revetted with sandbags. In the revetting, a slit had been made through which we could observe without being seen. For all that it was an uncomfortable place. Because of our restricted movement, when the call of nature came, the best we could do was to urinate into empty cans and then, with only our hands showing above the parapet, pour the contents on to the slope below.

We had come prepared for the long hours. We brought weapons, a number 38 wireless set, some tins of stew, tea and (what was as important - the means to warm our rations) lots of 'Tommy' cookers. These resembled the rings of camphor which were hung in wardrobes to deter moths. Their advantage was that, when ignited, they were smokeless, giving off an invisible vapour. Their disadvantage was that, in open wintry conditions, the heat they engendered was sufficient only to warm food. As for brewing tea, we spent most of the day in a futile effort to boil water in a mess tin. We used 'Tommy' cooker after 'Tommy' cooker until we had to admit failure. In disgust, we threw in the tea leaves, most of which floated. After some fruitless stirring, we produced an insipid and almost colourless concoction which we drank, tea leaves and all.

On a fourth night, patrolling gave place to a different undertaking. Two sections of 17 Troop, those of Jack and Tommy (the two experienced corporals), were to lay anti-personnel mines on what appeared to be a track leading up the slope towards the Marzolina positions. It was thought that it could be used as an approach by enemy patrols.

We set out through familiar territory towards the track. Familiar, too, were the sights and sounds of the night. Like sheet lightning, there were flashes and flares. Over to our left, like rolling thunder, we could hear the gunfire rumbling. Nearer to, the 'resident' Vickers and Spandau machine-guns exchanged fire over our heads.

As we lugged the rope-handled, heavy boxes of number 75 anti-personnel mines down to the track, from across the divide came the heart-rending and despairing cry, 'Heinrich! Heinrich! Heinrich!' The cry of an unfortunate German calling for the help of his comrade.

A fleeting feeling of compassion welled up inside me but in the front line there is little scope for compassion when circumstances militate towards the dulling of sensitivity. I turned my mind to the task in hand.

On reaching the track, we divided into groups: some to prime the mines; some to carry them, gingerly, to the chosen site; and just a pair of us to plant and bury them. Tommy, the other section's corporal, and I took on the meticulous task of planting the mines. We began a methodical and disciplined procedure. We knelt on the damp earth, side by side about two feet apart. First, working in unison, we dug a suitable hole with our hands. When the holes were ready, we acknowledged with a whisper. From a distance away, two primed mines were brought and planted simultaneously. Now came the delicate and dangerous task of covering the mines with soil until only the up-curving, sensitive flanges were visible. Knowing that even a slight touch of the flanges could detonate the mines and hampered by the darkness, with heightened tension, we carefully arranged the soil around the flanges, acknowledging again that we had finished the laying of two mines. Then, on our knees, again in unison, we moved backwards to repeat the drill all over again. It was a nerve-racking operation and, when all the mines had been laid, we plodded back drained of all nervous energy.

As the weather worsened, so aggressive activity by both sides diminished. We maintained nightly patrols as did the enemy parachutists whose patrols were mainly small in size. They were more likely to be of one or two men whose object was both to infiltrate into our forward defences and to seek information rather than engagement with our patrols. Occasionally, there was skirmishing. On one night, a patrol of ours penetrated the enemy defences and returned with four prisoners, the patrol commander reporting that five of the enemy had been killed. On the other hand, one of our patrols, of one officer and twelve men, failed to return and was subsequently reported missing.

The coming of the snows had been anticipated and had hastened the use of not only windproof clothing but also the wearing of white smocks for camouflage. At times they were an encumbrance but they gave added protection and warmth against the bitter cold. It was because temperatures were so low that the oiled moving parts of our weapons tended to freeze, so we resorted to graphite grease, the one lubricant which resisted the freezing conditions.

In the bitter cold, unit strength was steadfastly maintained. Only a trickle of men were reporting sick and had to leave the front line. Most of us remained reasonably healthy but battle weary. As for myself, the staphylococcus germ which had plagued me in warmer climes seemed to have been driven into hibernation by the cold. But, as the winter wore on, a new problem arose. I began to suspect that all was not well with the side of my left foot. It became numb and waxen white. It was time to visit JG, in his regimental aid post, at regimental headquarters. I was treated for the first stage of frost-bite. Daily, after each night of patrolling, I had to sit for a half-hour, with my affected foot in a bucket of warm, orange coloured liquid until the affected part became normal again. Ailments such as mine seemed to be affecting more and more of the regiment and we began to wonder whether we would ever be relieved. Now, the commitment of the 1st Division had extended to nearly three months and C Squadron was on Marzolina for another spell.

This tour was to be its last and the one in which misfortune struck 17 Troop. One of its patrols, during a skirmish with the enemy, had walked on to a minefield. Two of its most staunch and likeable soldiers suffered horrendous injuries. Jack, the rough diamond, who had led his section fearlessly through both the North African and the Italian campaigns, lost a leg and received serious wounds in the lower part of his body. 'Dinger', who would so well fit into the ranks of those who are called 'the salt of the earth', tragically lost both legs. Yet, both owed their lives to the very freezing conditions which daily we abhorred, cursed and railed against. As they were carried down the mountain slopes, the icy, cold conditions had the effect of coagulating the blood and sealing the bleeding stumps.

Sadly, for Jack and Dinger, our relief came just too late. On 11 January 1945, the regiment was relieved by two companies of Number 1 Battalion, 337 Regiment of the American 85th Division.

Our relief and that of the whole of 1st British Infantry Division was timely. After thirteen months of warfare, in which only six weeks of rest intervened, the division was deemed to be ready for rest and reorganization. Its war-weary soldiers were to leave Italy for the sun steeped, biblically famous, little country of Palestine.

We left behind the inhospitable mountains with their high sounding names of Monte Grande, Monte Cuccoli, Monte Farneto and Marzolina. Our armour we left at Borgo San Lorenzo, to be possessed by the returning and rested 46th Reconnaissance Regiment.

A journey by trucks brought us to our staging area, close to the Umbrian town of Perugia. Near to the outskirts, C Squadron was assigned to a large house. On my arrival with the advanced party, my first action was to seek the means of getting my filthy underclothing and towels washed. With this aim in mind, I crossed the valley between our quarters and the nearest houses. I found myself in a street named Via Annibale Vecchi. At Number 215, I knocked on the door. It was opened by a pretty, raven haired signorina. In my halting Italian, I made known my request. The signorina, Fernanda Carletti agreed that, on a reasonable payment, she would wash for me. When the rest of 16 Troop arrived, I persuaded her to wash for a few of my friends as well, enabling her to earn much needed money for herself and her extended family.

More than that, towards the end of our stay on the day before our departure, Fernanda's parents invited the four of us to share in an evening meal with all the family. During the afternoon, the grandfather had been out with his shotgun and returned with a bag of a dozen dead sparrows. These he plucked, beheaded and, without drawing their innards, impaled on a spit, to turn and roast them over the fire. Meanwhile, Fernanda and Mama had prepared a large bowl of salad, a mixture of lettuce, herbs and olives which had been drenched in olive oil. The meal, which was called *insalata*, was made ready and each of us sat down to a full plate of the salad, enhanced by the delicacy of roast sparrow.

Somewhat apprehensively, but instinctively, I seemed to have observed the right ritual of eating sparrow. I began to pick pieces of the dark, stringy flesh from the breast. Cockney George had no such qualms and, with his usual aplomb, attacked the carcass with gusto, leaving nothing much more than a skeleton and one or two pellets of lead shot. But, after washing down the meal with generous gulps of the traditional red wine, he appeared none the worse.

On the following morning, relaxed and with rising spirits, we prepared for the long journey by train down the length of the Italian peninsular to Taranto. Old French rolling stock awaited us at the station. The waggons bore the caption, '40 Hommes 4 Chevaux'. Inside 16 Troop's allotted waggon, the floor had been carpeted with straw; our communal bed and resting place for the two days of travel. On one side of the waggon were bullet holes and congealed blood stains, evidence that, formerly, the van had been under attack.

Lugging our kitbags, we climbed aboard, heavily laden in field service marching order. Soon, the floor of the van became a hotchpotch of sitting men and piles of equipment. At night, we lay in places so cramped for space that our legs criss-crossed in a kind of trellis pattern. For those who had to respond to the call of nature, it became an ordeal of disentangling legs and plotting a way over bodies to a heavy, sliding door which had to be left slightly ajar so that back spray caused by the slipstream of the speeding locomotive was deflected outwards.

At deserted places along the line, stops were made so that we could eat our pack rations and brew tea by simply using heated water from the engine's boiler. But for us, these conditions were sheer luxury when compared with our recent lot of winter warfare in the Apennines. More than that, there came the added pleasure of warm sunshine for, in Southern Italy, spring had arrived even though it was only mid-January.

When we reached the transit camp near Taranto, we were not allowed to relax. Immediately, Paddy began a campaign to smarten us up for the sea journey to Palestine. He was determined that his soldiers would march aboard as smart as on the day we landed in Italy, some thirteen months before. Hastily, we scrubbed clean our khaki coloured webbing equipment and then, with the application of white blanco, we affected a gleaming transformation. For attire, we were issued new khaki drill. In our kitbags, we hid away our muddied greatcoats and our soaked and sodden fighting boots which we replaced with our second more presentable and polished pair.

Thus smartened up, we dressed in field service marching order for Paddy's imposed inspection. On parade, we stood in ranks. At the front, our officers, unlike our loaded selves, were dressed only in uniforms with webbing belts. Paddy appeared in disgruntled mood and, after the inspection of his men, called over Clem, our squadron commander. In front of the ranks, he admonished him in these scathing words: 'If my men can appear in marching order, so can my officers. Have them paraded later, properly dressed as ordered. Dismiss the parade!'

On the following day, proudly and smartly, we embarked for the voyage. Calm seas prevailed throughout our sail. The skies were cloudless and under a warm sun we relaxed on deck. By night we slept soundly. There were regular, wholesome meals again. The battle seemed far away as the ship steamed eastwards. As darkness fell on the third evening, we saw the twinkling lights on Mount Carmel and then the harbour lights of Haifa. Palestine lay before us.

Quickly, on disembarkation, we were marshalled into a waiting train which rumbled slowly, throughout the night, towards Gaza in the south. By dawn, within a few miles of the town, we arrived at our destination; Camp 520 in the Number 21 Military Area.

Fourteen

The Fragile Peace

Camp 520 lay astride the road to Gaza. Apart from some impoverished plots of groundnut, the land on which it lay was treeless and barren. Within its perimeter fence – spaced out in lines and furnished with simple, low beds, canopied with mosquito nets – were the marquees of troopers and non-commissioned officers. For commissioned officers and administration offices there were wooden buildings dotted about the area. Into this new environment, with its dry heat and dust laden air, we began a life similar to that of a peacetime army unit on overseas commitment.

By day, drawn out by the heat of the sun, there was a persistent, pungent odour of dry, decomposed dung. But it was when the sun went down that, from distant orange groves, the cooling air became charged with and steeped in the heavy fragrance of orange blossom, its all pervading scent obliterating every undesirable odour.

The hot sun began to work its magic on our jaded, dampened-to-the-marrow bodies, on our winter pale skins and on our sodden clothing. Already, we felt looser in limb and supple in movement. The wan of our skin gave place to a healthy looking tan. The front of our greatcoats, still coated with the drying mud of Marzolina began to resemble, in miniature, the cracked surface of drought stricken land. The clinging lozenges of dried mud had to be picked off separately before a final brushing removed all traces. After a fortnight, our sodden battle boots were dry enough to absorb polish and, with constant brushing, developed an accepted shine again.

No sooner had we settled down in the encampment than regimentation began in earnest. Paddy, knowing more than we did of future operations, was determined that there would be no slackening off or lowering of standards in his fighting force. In place of the vicissitudes of winter warfare, there came the demand for high standards of smartness both of equipment and attire. His demand was best seen in the daily, guard-mounting ceremonies to which he added an attractive incentive. He would excuse all guard duties for any trooper who became commanding officer's stick orderly on three separate guard-mounting occasions.

This inducement brought deception and became lucrative for one or two 'old sweats'. They were the first to be excused all guards. To those who were prepared to pay for its usage, they began to loan their impeccable, gleaming brasses and their dazzling webbing equipment. For a while, they lined their pockets until others, not prepared for their services by dint of hours of work, brought their equipment up to a comparably high standard.

In every hour of the day, there were trumpet calls by which our daily life was ordered. On Paddy's initiative, bugles had been exchanged for cavalry trumpets. Their melodious sounds encouraged the lyricists to match words to music. For Reveille they chanted, 'Get up! Get up! You lazy beggars!' Sometimes, unwilling and fractious risers would alter the 'e' in beggars to a 'u'.

For the mail call, they mouthed the disrespectful words, 'Letters from Lousy Lily! Letters from Lousy Lou!'

At the calling out of the guard, they sang, 'Come and do a picket, boys! Come and do a guard!'

To the always welcome call for meals, with zest they sang, 'Come to the cookhouse door, boys! Come to the cookhouse door!'

On one occasion only, we heard the unfamiliar Fire Call. It came on a Sunday morning before Reveille was sounded. On the insistence of our non-commissioned officers, we rose reluctantly and hurriedly dressed. Then we were marched to the scene of the fire. Before us lay the charred and smoking remains of the wooden Officers' Mess. A few officers, in dressing gowns, stood gravely by, like Indian holy men officiating at a funeral rite. We, like spectators of the funeral pyre, stood at ease, unable to do anything to help. Our thoughts were more of breakfast than of a burnt-out building.

146

In March and April, the sun became hotter and more oppressive, forcing a different arrangement of our working day. At six in the morning we rose and, after breakfast and muster, we began our regular, daily maintenance of vehicles and weapons. In the heat of the day, enervated, we rested on our beds and sweated beneath our mosquito nets. To replace the heat we had lost through perspiration, we were expected to drink regularly from buckets of brine placed outside of the cookhouse. At the main meal of the day, under the watchful eye of the duty officer, each of us swallowed a yellow mepacrine tablet as a preventative against malaria. Its regular usage eventually gave us a jaundiced look.

For a while, when flies became pests, a new order was given. Before the main meal, each soldier had to bring along a matchbox containing the carcasses of twenty dead flies, a contribution which it was hoped would make inroads into the fly population. The exercise was soon abandoned when expectations were not realized and the legions of flies remained constant.

Frequent nights of guard duties, daily maintenance, the regular musters and the unremitting heat began to affect our demeanour. Tempers frayed, lethargy waxed and interest waned.

Relief from routine came when day trips were granted. 'Liberty' trucks provided a service to either Tel Aviv or Jerusalem. The opportunity to get away from Camp 520, if only for a day, was not lost. I made one visit only to Tel Aviv, a city which was the epitome of modernity. Its up-to-date buildings lined wide and busy main thoroughfares. It had modern cinemas showing modern films, a plethora of beer cellars and a well-used beach.

But lying on a beach was the least of my desires. With too much sun, my fair skin burned red and never became truly tanned. Along with Dinky, I turned my attention to a film matinée. We went to see the film of Ernest Hemmingway's book, *For Whom The Bell Tolls*. Because of my previous night's guard duty, before ten minutes had passed I had fallen into a deep sleep. According to Dinky, my head had dropped into the lap of a Jew at my side. As the show ended, he awakened me. Repentant and abashed, I rose to a sitting position and apologized for the inconvenience I had caused and thanked him for his tolerance.

Beer cellars and basement coffee houses abounded in the city centre and many of my peers used them as a means of escaping from the routine of Camp 520. But, in a country so historically endowed, I could see no point in whiling away the hours of leave in clammy beer cellars, on overcrowded streets and on sun-steeped beaches.

Jerusalem offered far more than Tel Aviv. I went there on several occasions in the early spring of 1945. My journey took me through the Judaean hills where the air seemed fresher than on the coastal plain. Spring flowers in abundance carpeted the slopes in a riot of colour. There was more pleasure still when the hills opened out and revealed the Old City of Jerusalem. There, above the honey-coloured walls, the dome of the Mosque of Omar gleamed golden in the morning sunshine. On the slopes below the walls, even the Arab gravestones, pointing uniformly towards Mecca, had caught the sun and spoke of life rather than death.

I started my pilgrimage at St Stephen's Gate and took a leisurely walk along the Via Dolorosa. Arab and Jew thronged the narrow thoroughfare without sign of hostility. From open, cavern-like shops, vendors plied their trade. There were a number of shops where bloodless meat, on hooks, hung down unprotected from numerous flies. Whiffs of its rawness irritated my nostrils.

My stroll ended at the Church of the Holy Sepulchre. Unimpressive from the outside, it was even less impressive on the inside. The sites of the Cross and Tomb were on different levels. A hole in the floor marked the place of the Crucifixion, a marble tomb denoted the place of the Resurrection. On view, close to the site of the Cross, in a glass case, was the figure of the Madonna, bedecked in £2,000,000 worth of jewellery.

Emerging into the bright sunlight, I made my way through the Damascus Gate. Outside the city walls, I found Gordon's Tomb in a beautiful, well-tended garden. Not far away was the outcrop of rock called Golgotha, known as the Place of the Skull because of its skull-like resemblance. Here, in these natural surroundings, I could not help but think of how they matched up to my boyhood imaginations and the bible texts that I had read.

At the Wailing Wall, this one remaining wall of Solomon's Temple, I met two Palestine policemen who told me they were there to guard against desecration of the wall by Arabs who sometimes urinated down from the precincts of the Mosque of Omar. In the passage below and standing close to the Wall,

Orthodox bearded Jews in sombre clothing intoned and swayed. In the cracks between the massive blocks of stone were stuffed papers bearing prayers and petitions.

On a further visit, I joined a guide-led party on Mount Zion. At the Church of the Galligantu (the cock crowing), as I entered the domed building, I marvelled at its interior. The dome and the walls had been beautifully and colourfully decorated in mosaics. As we stood with our backs against one wall, we were asked to turn round. There on the wall was an uneven, bare patch which begged for an explanation. The guide told us that all the work in mosaic had been accomplished by one monk in a lifetime of devotion and skill. He had died before its completion. The bare patch had been left as his memorial.

As soon as we were able, my friends and I chose to go on a trip by bus to the Dead Sea. The bus carried us from Jerusalem, through Bethany, down the long, winding valley towards Jericho. On either side, we were hemmed in by rugged, rocky hills which like the increasing heat seemed overpowering. Then, at over 2,000 feet below normal sea level, we arrived at a watering place on the shore of the Dead Sea.

In the cubicles of a waterside building, we prepared to bathe in brine of such density that floating on the surface of the sea was the most we could do. Swimming or splashing about was undesirable and would have caused irritation and smarting of the eyes. But of our buoyancy there was no doubt and what we had heard from second-hand information had now been proved. On our leaving the briny waters, the effect of sun's power on our bodies evaporated the moisture at once, leaving them coated with irritating salt crystals which we flushed off under fresh water showers. When we dressed again, our clothing became clammy with perspiration and we were glad to leave the oppressive heat of the Dead Sea region for the climb upwards to Jerusalem where the air was fresher and less enervating.

But, it was away from the historic centres of tourism where I found my greatest pleasures. There were sites of biblical moment which I came across by chance. Once, in order to have gunnery practice, I found myself, in a heavy armoured car, riding through the Judaean hills, south-west of Jerusalem. At a Palestine Police Force post, near the entrance to a large valley, I learned with great interest that the car was about to pass through the Valley of Elan, the historic site of David's encounter with Goliath.

In the time of my awaiting to start the gunnery practice, I gazed up the valley, overshadowed on either side by hills and spurs. Below their slopes, in the valley bottom, a rough track followed the line of a winding, dried-up bed of a stream. In my mind's eye, I saw that scene of long ago when the armies of Israelites and Philistines faced each other across the divide; and I heard the shouts and sounds of war.

Now, thousands of years later, the valley was, again, to resound to the noises of warfare for, on the slopes to the left and right of the track, derelict vehicles were to receive a pounding from my 37mm cannon as the armoured car moved through the valley. Unlike the outcome of the victorious battle when David slew Goliath, the gunnery practice was not successful. The track was not only bumpy and rough but also my firing on the move was disappointing. It was extremely difficult, in a brief moment, to hit a target while turning a manually operated gun turret through ninety degrees in a car that was moving. But, after all my efforts, I was more than compensated by coming to the ancient biblical site.

I well remember my first visit to the Mount of the Beatitudes from which there were wonderful views across the beautiful, blue Sea of Galilee and, looking landward, the view of Capernaum and its ruined temple. I found great enjoyment and peace as I sat among the spring flowers and grasses, reflecting that here, Jesus Christ must have walked and talked and preached the Sermon on the Mount.

I was glad that I had been brought to the Holy Land and had seen some of its beauty and ancient history. The real reason I was there, however, was that I was part of a force sent there for military reasons, which will become clear as the story unfolds.

Fifteen

Internal Security Operations

With the end of the war in Europe, significant happenings occurred which were to end the Regiment's stay in Camp 520 and to herald a new role in its operations. First, a misunderstanding between France and Syria was prompted by an agreement which had been reached during the war. Because of Syria's co-operation in the war effort, France would cease to hold sovereignty and would grant Syria autonomy. The Arabs wanted an immediate withdrawal of all French troops to the Lebanon. For the Arabs, the pace of withdrawal seemed too slow and, consequently, there was unrest both in Damascus and in the hills of the Syrian Jebel Druzes. In response to this unrest, the French began to shell Damascus from the fort at Mezze, some miles from the city.

As a result, the 1st Infantry Division was placed on an immediate operational footing and given the task of coaxing French Army units westwards into the Lebanon. This new venture engendered feelings of expectancy, excitement and apprehension such as those of earlier campaigns.

Under two hours' notice to move we, in C squadron, began a frenzied rearming and servicing of our armour. By evening, we began to roll northwards towards the Syrian-Palestine border. A night of driving brought us into the Galilean hills from where, at dawn, we saw the sun rise majestically over the blue waters of the Sea of Galilee. In low gear, on a downward, winding road, we came to Tiberias, from where we began a steep climb upwards, past Capernaum, until we reached the border post of Rosh Pinna.

We entered Syria on a flat road bordered by land strewn haphazardly with boulders as if some giant, in a frenzy, had hurled them everywhere. On almost every boulder, there seemed to be a lizard basking in the now hot sunshine.

Tension began to rise as 16 Troop's heavy armoured cars approached the fort of Mezze. A winding track led upwards towards its walls. There was no noise or movement on its battlements. The troop commander decided that he would advance slowly up the track. So, with hatches down, the car ascended, he observing through his periscope and I with eyes pressed against the telescopic sights of the gun, my right hand on the pistol-like firing grip. Our movement upwards brought no immediate response until, suddenly, from out of the gates of the fort, travelling at speed, came a truckload of troops. Through the 'inter-communication' set, came the troop commander's orders:

'Gun, traverse left-steady, on!'

The truck loomed large in my sights and I was ready to destroy both it and its occupants. I awaited the order of 'Fire'. It never came. Through his periscope, the troop commander had observed that the troops were unarmed French Senegalese, wearing red fezzes. In his wisdom, he allowed them to pass by and ride into the waiting hands of the follow-up troops while he kept the fort under surveillance.

Soon, both the fort and an adjacent airfield were in our hands and the immediate task was complete. But, by the next morning, new orders had reached C Squadron. Along with an infantry company of the Duke of Wellington's Regiment, it was to take part in an expedition to the hilly stronghold of the Syrian Jebel Druze, its objective being a French Foreign Legion barracks on the outskirts of the Druze region.

News had reached the military authorities that the Druzes had forcefully ejected a regiment of French Cavalry and a battalion of Legionnaires. Furthermore, an armoured car and large amounts of small-arms ammunition had been stolen.

There were reports that the Mountain Druzes were an exclusive, warlike people who took offence at the intrusion into their territory. More than that, rumour had it that they were ruled by a White Queen. So, our immediate orders were to enter only the villages on the periphery of the region, seeking only the armoured car and the missing ammunition.

We set off across a hot, arid plain – passing one or two small, isolated, crumbling, clay-walled forts – until we reached the deserted, French outpost. We were astonished at the amount of wanton destruction. The windows in the barrack blocks were not only devoid of glass but also were stripped of their wooden casements. In short, we had found the empty shell of a barracks. Debris was strewn everywhere. In the Legionnaires cemetery, the gravestones had been vandalized and, from the simple stone crosses, all the oval, metal name plaques had been removed, mixed up and piled in an untidy heap. One grave had been opened and desecrated.

Clem, the squadron commander, decided that we would occupy the barrack buildings and its surrounds as a base of operations. Our armoured cars were positioned round the perimeter. In case of a night attack, the cars' searchlights were set ready to cast their beams outwards. Guards were doubled and we slept in snatches, lying beside our armour. Morning came without any resort to action.

Soon, sections of armoured cars set out to explore distant villages. In the troop commander's car, we moved off to what we thought was an Arab village called Chaaba. We expected to see a number of simple houses or hovels. Instead, to our amazement, we found Arab dwellings scattered within ancient ruins. These, we discovered later, were of the Greco-Roman period and the site was that of Phillipopolis, one of the cities of the Decapolis.

Our approach was by a road still paved in places with the original, heavy Roman paving stones. As we advanced further into the site, we came across the ruined, pillared area of the forum and, not far away, a small amphitheatre. In its arcades, Arab families were dwelling.

Down a sandy thoroughfare, we found the Muktar's house. He came out to meet the troop commander and, in a gesture of friendship, invited both him and his driver to go indoors, to sit cross-legged on a carpet, to parley and to sip black coffee from tiny glasses. As usual, I was denied taking part in the formalities and remained in the turret to maintain wireless communication.

But, later, I was rewarded when the Muktar took me down the sandy track to what appeared to be a ramshackle hut. Inside, there were two Arabs leaning on besoms. At the Muktar's command, they began a feverish brushing aside of the inches-deep layer of sand beneath their feet. Underneath, in all its pristine splendour, lay a beautiful, mosaic Greco-Roman bathroom floor. I believed that I was gazing at a sight few Westerners had seen.

Our visit to the village was memorable but there was neither sign nor information of the stolen armoured car and ammunition. Another patrol was more successful having found some ammunition and the armoured car. It was discovered that, sensibly, the French car crew had removed the breach block of the car's cannon and so rendered it useless.

Before our withdrawal from the area, Clem sent a strong message to the headman of the nearest village, ordering him to send some of his men to clear up the debris in the barracks. But Arab men do not do such menial tasks and the response was a message bearing the lame excuse that all the men were on guard duty. It was a polite, face-saving answer.

So we left the ruined barracks and began patrolling westwards into the Bekaa valley, skirting Baalbek and its historic ruins, regrettably having no time to stop and stare. On we went, driving upwards, along winding roads, past cedar-topped hills and down seaward facing slopes to Beirut. In the city, we parked our armour in the Place Des Canons. There was time only for a stroll along the sea front. Our assignment was over. All the French forces were now in the Lebanon. We returned to Syria, to encamp for a short period on the slopes of Mount Hermon. There we learned that new dispositions had been planned by the army command. First British Infantry Division was to leave Number 21 Military Area and move northwards to be deployed in Number 15 Military Area which bordered on Southern Lebanon. Its place in the south would be taken by the incoming 6th Airborne Division.

The arrival of the Red Berets presaged the news that both divisions would be taking part in the invasion of Japan. Strategically, both were nearly halfway to the Pacific theatre of war. Both were experienced; the one in airborne assault, the other in seaborne landings.

The first sign of our participation came with the preparation of a regimental advance party destined for Colombo, in Ceylon. We, in the ranks, began to look on the coming operation with foreboding, particularly when we learned that the Allies could expect heavy casualties. In my own gloomy thoughts, for the first time, I could think of no way of my surviving a third campaign.

At the same time, to exacerbate my melancholy, the staphylococcus germ had begun a further assault on my person, manifesting itself in a crop of boils. JG's response was to send me to a field hospital. There, a sample of pus was taken in a vain effort to create a vaccine. In the end, I returned painfully with a shot of penicillin in my rear.

In the time I was absent from duty, there came happenings of great import. Atom bombs fell on the Japanese cities of Hiroshima and Nagasaki. Within hours Japan had capitulated. Thousands of Japanese had died. Thousands more were casualties but hundreds of thousands more of both Japanese and Allied lives had been saved. In the 1st Reconnaissance Regiment, our former celebrations of VE Day could not match our overwhelming joy and relief felt at the end of the Second World War.

The end of hostilities was the beginning of a tour of duty under the auspices of The League Of Nations and under the mandate of Britain to keep the peace in Palestine. The fragile peace the men of 1st British Infantry Division had enjoyed for six months was over. Millions of Jews were clamouring for a homeland. Extracts from the Balfour Declaration of 1922 were being quoted out of context. The extract, 'The British Government views with favour the establishment of a National Home for Jews in Palestine,' was not followed by the following extract, 'it being clearly understood that nothing shall prejudice the civil and religious rights of non-Jewish communities in Palestine.'

British land and sea forces were there to uphold the mandate, to protect the rights of Jew and Arab and, what was anathema to the Jew, to strictly control by quota the numbers of Jews coming to settle in Palestine.

The frustration of the Jews manifested itself both in attempts at illegal entry by sea, and in the emergence of the terrorist organizations Hagana and Irgun Zvai Leumi.

Counter-terrorist operations began and, because of its mobility, the regiment became part of the Internal Security Force, being at two hours' notice to move to trouble spots. Encounters with the men of violence began as soon as the regiment began to move to its new station at Rosh Pinna close to the border. It was soon to suffer its first casualty. The happening occurred as B Squadron's men and armour were being transported by rail to the port of

Haifa. The rolling stock was assembled in two parts. At the front of the train were the carriages for the men. In the rear were 'flats', each carrying an armoured car anchored and secured by ropes. On each flat, guards were stationed. At the approach to Haifa station there was an incline. As the train moved slowly up the slope, the terrorists, unseen, uncoupled the flats from the carriages. The flats began to move backwards, gradually gathering speed down the incline. The resulting collisions and derailments snapped the securings of the armoured cars. It was then that Brad, a corporal, was crushed to death between two of the vehicles.

The atrocity generated seething anger in the ranks of the regiment. Here was a comrade who had survived two campaigns, who had fought alongside the Jewish Brigade in Italy, and who had fought so that both Jews and the world's people should be free of tyranny only to lose his life in such a diabolical act.

Brutal acts against unarmed soldiers had already taken place. One such act was against two sergeants of the Royal Engineers. They were found hanged and strung upside down in an orange grove.

Before long, the terrorists struck again; fortunately, on this occasion, without causing death. Paddy, the regimental commander, was for once caught off his guard. He was abducted from a hotel in Naharyia, a coastal town. He was taken away, stripped to his underpants and brutally beaten. He returned alone, his back marked with great weals. Again, in the regiment, anger and feelings of revenge arose but the discipline and control of a fighting regiment prevailed.

At Rosh Pinna, we began a tour of duty in which there was constant patrolling; searches for caches of arms in remote kibbutzim and protection of civil Administrators. The Assistant District Commissioner, residing by day in Safed, sought refuge each night in the regimental encampment. Occasionally, the night hours were disturbed by bursts of machine-gun fire. Streams of bullets would pass over our vulnerable marquees. There would be a hurried stand to arms and foot patrols would go out to seek the gunmen who had disappeared under cover of darkness.

To maintain control in the stony, wild and hilly border country, Paddy formed a cavalry troop, its horsemen making frequent patrols in areas denied to our armour. The additional trumpet calls of Stables, which sounded before Reveille, began to further disturb our rest.

It was while the regiment continued its operations that the most foul atrocity of all took place. A wing of the splendid King David Hotel in Jerusalem was demolished by a huge explosion. The wing contained the headquarters of British troops in Palestine. Loss of life was so great that over 100 staff, both men and women, were killed.

The carnage was the result of a 'Gunpowder Plot' which, unlike the infamous Gunpowder Plot of British history, succeeded where the first had failed. It was conceived and implemented after covert observation of the daily servicing of the hotel. Each morning, at ten o'clock, a truck, manned and driven by Arabs in traditional dress, delivered churns of milk which were unloaded and rolled down a slope into the basement. On the morning of the dastardly deed, at nine-thirty instead of ten o'clock, the terrorists, disguised as Arabs and riding in an identical truck, began to unload and roll down the churns. Instead of milk, they were packed with explosives. Soon after the perpetrators had left and before the arrival of the bona fide truck, the wing of the hotel and the service men and women were no more.

Within two hours, a strong force of our armoured cars was despatched southwards to Tel Aviv. There, road-blocks were established on all roads entering the city. Our light armoured cars began a patrol of the empty, silent streets, our Bren guns at the ready as the infantry of the division began an ordered search for terrorists, explosives and arms. Whether or not the operation was a success we were not to know, for after two days we were ordered back to Rosh Pinna.

There, I was made aware that I would be returning to the United Kingdom for a month's leave under a scheme with the abbreviation of LIAP (Leave in advance of Python), Python being the code-word for demobilization.

Sixteen

Diversions From Duty

After close on three years away from my homeland I found
myself, on Christmas Eve of 1945, in Port Said where I
embarked on an American ship, the *Medina Victory*. I boarded in
high spirits for my first Christmas at sea. The ship left that
evening, sailing westwards on a calm sea into a most glorious
sunset. But there was no warning of what was to come. Below
deck, on bunks tiered four high and two feet apart, sleep came
sweetly and quickly for all.

On Christmas morning, when I awoke, I was soon to realize
that the calm of the night before had given way to a fierce storm
and mountainous seas. The Mediterranean Sea, more often at its
level best, now seemed at its roughest worst. As I lay, I could
tolerate the heavy pitching and rolling of the ship. It seemed that
others, lying in their bunks, could not and were already spraying
the deck floor below with their vomit.

I decided that I would make the effort to rise and wash. As I
dropped down from my top bunk and landed on the deck floor,
immediately I was made aware of the violence of the storm. The
ship was pitching and rolling at the same time. When she pitched,
her screw rose out of the water. There was tremendous vibration
until the propeller fell back and bit on the water again. When she
rolled, loose objects slid along the deck floor.

I staggered to the ablutions area and began to draw water into
the sink. The water began to swirl round the bowl like a whirlpool.
I retched without vomiting but I was unable to face the wash. I
made my way up to the mess deck in the vain hope that getting
something down may be better than throwing something up. As I
stood at the entrance to the mess deck, a solitary, nauseated being,

I saw a remarkable but absurd scene. Two hundred hard boiled eggs rolled round the tables, following each other as if the devil would take the hindmost. I left the eggs to their gyrations and struggled back to my bunk, where I was to stay until evening. Meanwhile, hatches had been battened down on the upper deck and the atmosphere below became oppressively hot, the stench of vomit overpowering.

The first sign that there was someone steering the ship came from the bridge when, over the ship's tannoy system, a voice announced that the cooks would endeavour to provide a Christmas evening meal. When the time came, I groggily made my way to the mess deck. A seedy looking few were already seated. I collected my meal, sat down and, while the ship pitched and rolled, I managed to eat my slices of turkey. The vegetables and stuffing I consigned to the bin knowing that at least they would not be wasted on the denizens of the deep.

Another night of storm was followed by a morning when both the ship's company and we, the passengers, began to struggle towards normality. The first indication that everyone would have to 'pull himself together' came when the ship's captain announced that an inspection of sleeping quarters would be made later that morning. So, with mops and buckets, the cleansing of vomit-spattered floors began followed by the folding of rumpled blankets and dishevelled clothing. Then the examination of the sleeping deck was carried out to the satisfaction of a queasy looking captain.

It was on the third day that the *Medina Victory* reached the coastal waters of southern France. By then the storm had abated enough to allow the hatches to be opened and, for the first time since leaving Egypt, soldiers were allowed on the upper deck. In the bright sunlight, and breathing the pure fresh air again, they watched as the ship entered the port of Toulon.

In Toulon, having regained a normal gait rather than splayed sea legs, I boarded a train travelling northwards, at night, by an electrified rail system. The train hurtled through the night at speeds I had not experienced on British steam trains. By morning, I had reached the big transit camp in Dieppe. By sea I travelled to Newhaven and then on by train to my home town of Macclesfield.

My homecoming and my month's leave were an anticlimax. My

long absence had so separated me from the life I had known before that I never really adjusted to the comforts and freedom it offered. Virtually a boy when I left home, I returned a man. The vicissitudes of warfare had dulled my sensitivity and hardened me physically. At night, my body took unkindly to the mattress and sheets. I slept less well than I had done when lying on the earth wrapped in a single blanket between the coverings of my groundsheet and gas cape.

More than that, I found that I had returned to a nation whose peoples were still in the grip of austerity. The gaiety and verve of pre-war Britain had yet to resurface even though the war had ended. Most of my peers, both male and female, were still serving in the armed forces so, in my rounds of visiting, I met mostly older relatives and friends. Repertory and films provided most of my entertainment but, once, I went to an all-stars football match at the Maine Road ground of Manchester City Football Club. I had a good reason for going there. I wanted to see Frank Swift, England's international goalkeeper, who became the 1st Reconnaissance Regiment's physical training instructor when it was encamped in Norfolk.

Both on and off duty, good rapport had developed between Frank and myself. On the one hand, both because of his great height and strength and because of my shortness of stature and weight, in physical training, in a friendly way, I became his 'whipping boy'. For demonstrations of certain exercises, he singled me out, easily throwing me about in moves which I did not mind for he had huge, safe hands which never allowed me to fall.

On the other hand, when home leave came round, both of us were forced to make a tedious journey by train, across the country towards Manchester, changing trains twice before reaching home. Always, when we changed trains at Peterborough North station, Frank, of the generous heart, would let neither fame or rank keep him from buying tea and snacks for me.

Even after the football match, when I waved my beret and shouted from my stand seat, Frank returned the compliment, smiled knowingly and waved in return. Sadly, I was not to see him again for, in 1953, he met a tragic death in the Munich air disaster.

On my return for further duty in the Middle East and before

demobilization, I was given two further short leaves in Egypt. Both were interrupted by happenings which could not be anticipated. On my arrival in Cairo for a five-day leave, Ahmed Pasha, Egypt's Prime Minister, was assassinated. There was turmoil in the streets and, by orders of the army command, all British soldiers were confined to their hostels. We, in our small, claustrophobic guest house, spent three days before we were allowed out of confinement. It was only on the last day of leave that we were able to see a limited number of sights including the Blue Mosque and the Museum of Anthropology.

A second, short leave was spent in a services holiday camp near Lake Timsah and not far from Ishmalia. All activities were confined to the camp. No one was allowed to visit the town because an outbreak of bubonic plague had placed it out of bounds.

But the most significant happening of the year 1946 occurred before my demobilization at the end of that year.

Seventeen

The Demise of the Regiment

The signs were there already. Sixteen Troop was beginning to disintegrate. The first to leave was one of its stalwarts, the irrepressible Cockney George. His civilian occupation had qualified him for B release. As a milk roundsman, he had been categorized an agricultural worker. He was soon to deliver milk to Lambeth Palace again. Dinky, of the Bicycle Club, a staunch friend, left the troop bound for Egypt and a new role, instructing in the use of explosives.

But of greater import in the breaking up of the regiment was the departure of Paddy, our regimental commander. He was to become brigade major in the 6th Airborne Division. I remember well my seeing him for the last time. We came face to face on a camp roadway. I saluted as he passed by. Then, I was surprised to hear him call me by name. I turned and we shook hands. Although I was one of his wireless operators with whom he had had little contact, I knew that all his wireless operators held a special place in his estimation, being important components in the success of his command.

After Paddy's departure, and for the remaining time of the regiment's existence, Long John took command. He led the remnant of the regiment from Palestine into Egypt. There, in a huge camp, at Fayid in Egypt, the 1st Reconnaissance Regiment lost its identity. Its remaining soldiers were transferred to a regular army cavalry regiment, the 4/7th Dragoon Guards. Disbandment was complete.

Battle honours inscribed on regimental colours or regimental silver displayed in officers' messes and in regimental depots, perpetuating long years of tradition; these were not to be its

162

legacy. For some time yet its deeds, its honours and its *esprit de corps* will be commemorated in the hearts and minds of its living, veteran soldiers. They will remember its valiant dead (some 120 warriors), its wounded and those who returned and have died in the ensuing years. Perchance their memory will be kept alive in this written tribute.

Postscript

On my joining the 4/7th Dragoon Guards, I was posted to the headquarters signal troop. Preparations were being made for the return to Palestine to take on the role of the disbanded 1st Reconnaissance Regiment at Rosh Pinna. I became one in an advanced party of three Daimler Dingo armoured cars which set off to cross the Sinai Desert and the Negev to Beersheba and then on through Judaea to our destination.

It was not an easy journey. In searing desert heat our troubles began. Tyre pressures began to mount. The answer was to drive for short spells and to stop, open the tyre valves and relieve the pressure of the expanding air. On our climbing and ascending a mid-Sinai range of hills, further troubles hindered us. Tyres began to rupture and all spare tyres were used. By the time we had crossed the desert further blow-outs compelled us to leave one car and its crew behind, robbing the vehicle of its wheels and propping it up to await help from those following.

At Beersheba, cars and crews stopped for a rest close to a walled, military cemetery of the First World War. Inside its high walls were the graves of soldiers of General Allenby's 53rd Welsh Division. Apart from the graves of Welsh soldiers, I came across the resting places of men of the Cheshire Regiment, my own county regiment.

On leaving Beersheba, the heat of the day began to subside and we progressed quickly through the familiar territory of Judaea, to reach the camp at Rosh Pinna as darkness fell.

Here the days and weeks passed by until, in September of 1946, five years after my call-up, the process of demobilization began. A fortnight before I left, I was offered promotion. Whether this offer was a sop to encourage me to sign for service in the regular army, I did not know. I knew only that, on the one hand, I would lose a particular and wholesome camaraderie which had been nurtured and developed in peril and hardship.

On the other hand, I would be returning to my beloved land; to leave behind for ever the staphylococcus germ, to live in a temperate climate more suited to my fair-skinned inheritance, and to enjoy the seasonal verdant greens of a rain-washed isle rather than the browns and umbers of sun-scorched lands. I refused promotion and the possibility of rapid progress through the ranks. I was ready for home.

On the eve of my departure a party was held, a kind of 'send off' gathering. I was toasted in the Egyptian-made 'Stella' beer. My comrades drank to the point of drunkenness but I was determined not to reach a state which might cause me to miss the early-morning mail truck to Haifa.

So, shortly after Reveille, by courtesy of the post corporal, I lay in the back of the truck, atop mail bags, being buffeted about as the vehicle bounced and swayed down rough, hilly roads to Haifa. From there, I took a train travelling southwards by the coastal plain of Palestine. Eventually, I reached my destination, the transit camp at Alexandria.

For several days I remained there and became aware of increasing hostility towards British troops. A tide of nationalism was sweeping away the once firm sands of Anglo-Egyptian co-operation. Chanting students roamed through the main thoroughfares of Alexandria demanding that the British military presence be ended. At the gates of the transit camp, to warn against the perils of leaving camp, large notices cautioned troops not only that they go out in groups of two or more but also that pick helves 'must be carried for personal protection.'

On my last day in the transit camp, I was strolling between marquees when suddenly, behind me, I heard a familiar voice, one I had heard many times before and expected never to hear again. I was greeted with the words, 'Wotcha! Young Niss! How the hell are yer!'

I turned and, incredibly, I saw that Cockney George was back and exercising his will again. Six months before, on early release, he had left the 1st Reconnaissance Regiment. Now, disillusioned with civilian life and missing the camaraderie of army life, he had returned for a regular army commitment with the 15/19th Hussars.

With a twinge of nostalgia, I wished him well as I fought off a rising feeling that I wanted to join him. But, later, with the words of Cockney George ringing in my ears, I boarded the ship, bound for my native land.

I was not to see Cockney George again. He died in 1994. For fourteen years, he served in the 15/19 Hussars. In that time, he rose to the rank of squadron sergeant-major. At the end of his military service, he became an usher in the Houses of Parliament. Deservedly, he was awarded the British Empire Medal. At his funeral, as a token of their esteem, several Members of Parliament and forty service men of his regiment paid their tributes.

I know of few better words with which to honour my wartime friend and comrade than those of William Wordsworth taken from his poem, 'Character of the Happy Warrior'. They read,

> Who is the happy warrior? Who is he
> That every man in arms should wish to be?
> It is the generous Spirit, who when brought
> Among the tasks of real life, hath wrought
> Upon a plan that pleased his boyish thought:
> Whose high endeavours are an inward light
> That makes the path before him always bright:
> Who if he rise to station of command,
> Rises by open means; and there will stand
> On honourable terms, or else retire,
> And in himself possess his own desire.

Eighteen

Views from the Slit Trench

I think it is fair to write that the troopers of the 1st Reconnaissance Regiment, for the larger part of their campaigning, fought in slit trenches at the side of the infantry battalions, rather than in their armoured vehicles following their designated role of reconnaissance. This supposition seems to have been borne out in the appendix of the book, *This Band Of Brothers*, a history of the Reconnaissance Corps.

In the form of percentages, it was ascertained that 12 percent only of time was spent in reconnaissance, 9 percent in protection, 34 percent acting as infantry and 45 percent in an obscure category of miscellaneous and concentrated.

A following paragraph states:

Although willing to take on any reconnaissance job, however difficult, the corps found itself hampered by the lack of heavy armour and fire power in support of the Bren carriers and cars. The introduction of the heavier (medium) armoured car, mounting a 37mm gun was a partial solution (on the Anzio Beach head, the medium armoured cars achieved success in repelling German infantry attacks), but regiments were happy to have attached, as occurred on occasions, 75mm guns mounted on half tracks (on the Anzio Beach Head it was mostly the splendid 25-pounder guns which gave close support) and some American self-propelled 105mm guns (at Anzio, these were co-ordinated under an extensive plan of Army Group, Royal Artillery).

In North Africa, where the 1st Reconnaissance Regiment took

part in vicious fighting near Medjez El Bab, it became evident that, in General Von Armin's strategy of using concentrated tank formations, the regiment's armour was no match for them. Furthermore, at that time, neither the supporting Churchill tanks nor the Regiment's six-pounder anti-tank guns were fully effective, being out-gunned and out-ranged by the enemy's Mark Four tank.

A further hazard faced the Regiment – the German Teller mine. Its eleven pounds of the high explosive, Tolite, was devastating to our lightly armoured vehicles. A quarter-inch-thick armour was no protection. The low slung Bren carriers, in particular, were death traps for drivers and commanders. Sand bags packed in the bottom of the carriers were ineffective. At the beginning, 15 cwt trucks carrying the assault troops' riflemen were vulnerable to small arms fire and were replaced by American Scout cars with armoured sides.

Smaller lessons were learned from captured enemy material. Of great value was the German four-gallon petrol can – the Jerry can. It was better than our own two-gallon can. As well as holding twice as much petrol it had a cap which was incorporated into an excellent non-screw locking device. Small wonder that the Allies copied and produced their own Jerry cans.

In the heat of the African sun, I envied the soldiers of the Afrika Korps who wore a forage cap with an elongated peak which made a most effective shade for the face. My khaki beret protected the head only and I regretted that my fair, sensitive skin had no such protection.

But it was in Italy that the role of the regiment, for the most part, was that of specialist infantry. This role brought its problems for the men. Certainly, the regiment's firepower more than matched that of an infantry battalion, but, on the other hand, in manpower its troopers numbered perhaps less than a third of an infantry battalion's riflemen. This deficiency was exacerbated in the scout troops by the ratio of one non-commissioned officer for every two troopers. Even the assault troops had two non-commissioned officers for every five riflemen.

When holding the line, the lack of numbers on the ground placed a heavy strain on troopers. Gunners, wireless operators, and drivers were all active both on the beach head and in the later mountain warfare, where night patrolling was frequent and added fatigue to strain. This dearth of manpower is confirmed in earlier chapters of this book where it can be read that I was continually being seconded from 16 Troop to one of 17 Troop's assault sections.

The personal story of the Anzio campaign is written in an earlier chapter. From my own limited experience of the battle; from a study of some of the post-war commentaries; and in reply to the criticism, controversy and condemnation of the direction and execution of the landing, I make my own appraisal.

It seems that the heaviest burden of blame for a campaign which some have called a failure was apportioned to one man: General John Lucas, commander of the 6th American Corps during the initial stages of the campaign. The only blame I would apportion to General Lucas would not be for his hesitation and caution but for his acceptance of a task which charged him to make a seaborne, initial assault with two infantry divisions and a relatively small force of armour and a small group of specialist troops. His experience in the earlier landings at Salerno - when two army corps, one British and one American, were hard put to get off the beaches - ought to have been enough to persuade him to refuse the command of such a small landing force.

Certainly, General Lucas had the backing and support of a powerful naval force and near supremacy in the air, but it was with a limited force of infantry and armour that the assault would have to be made. (Conjecturally, the question is asked - would a Montgomery or a Patten have accepted the task without the initial landing of an additional strong and mobile armoured force?)

Two factors seemed to have affected the course of the landing: the strength of the landing force and the contingency plans of the German High Command in Italy.

With regard to the first factor, again conjecturally. Because of paucity in weight of numbers and armour, had the assaulting divisions forged ahead there could have ensued a bloody and perhaps more unacceptable outcome than what really happened.

The second factor is confirmed in the memoirs of General Albert von Kesselring, the commander in chief of the German Army Group South. His contingency plans seem to lend support both to the supposition above and to the argument in favour of a cautious build-up favoured by General Lucas.

Kesselring, in his book, reveals the extent to which he went in order to oppose Allied seaborne landings. There seems no doubt that he expected the Allies to attempt a landing, particularly in view of their erstwhile problems in breaking through the Gustav Line in the south. The threat of a seaborne landing increased so much so that Kesselring had even earmarked the area surrounding Rome, from Civitavecchia to Gaeta, as a probable site.

With this area in mind, in event of a landing, he had planned a speedy convergence of troops into the battle zone. Initially, two divisions would be drawn from General Von Manstein's 14th Army in Northern Italy. From outside of Italy, he would quickly move the 114th, Jaager Rifle Division from Yugoslavia. From Army Group West and from Ober Kommand Wehrmacht in Germany, he had already arranged a quick transfer of divisions and specialist élite formations.

The two factors can now be placed in the context of the seaborne landings, code-named 'Operation Shingle', which began early in the morning of Saturday 22 January 1944 and were virtually unopposed. But, at once, both Lucas and Kesselring had their anxieties. On the one hand, Lucas feared an immediate counter-attack, an expectancy which was to be confirmed for, on the other hand, Kesselring writes in his memoirs that he had planned an immediate counter-attack that very day, only to find that his plan had been 'incomprehensibly and arbitrarily altered' by his subordinate commanders even though battalion after battalion had been rushed as far south as possible for the purpose.

But, early on the first day, he had acted quickly by ordering Von Pohl, his 'flak' commander, to surround the beach head with a ring of 88mm gun batteries which would be hard for tanks to penetrate (it seems that Kesselring had expected a heavily armoured force to land).

Into the gaps between the emplaced gun batteries, piecemeal as they arrived, he placed battle elements of several divisions. Thus, as enemy resistance to the Allied advance strengthened so it became more difficult for General Lucas to maintain forward momentum. In the British sector alone, General Penney of the 1st British Infantry Division had, eventually, to commit his only reserve, the gallant 3rd Infantry Brigade, in an attempt to secure the objectives of Campoleone station and the Osterraccia crossroads. Meanwhile, in the American sector, the 3rd American

Division was attempting to capture Cisterna and to cut Highway Seven. Neither objective was achieved.

With each passing day, the counter-attacking battalions of seven German divisions and their supporting armour began to reduce the Allied salient. Fierce and bloody battles were fought until, at last, the enemy counter-attacks foundered on the unyielding defences of the Allied infantry holding the Corps defence line. Now, any attempt to advance by either of the exhausted antagonists was out of the question. For four months, they were to face each other across a no man's land reminiscent of the First World War battles in France.

Once again, the appraisal becomes conjectural. Would an initial three-Divisional lift of two infantry divisions with the addition of the 1st American Armoured Division have succeeded? It may have done with a changed plan of attack. Instead of seizing Campoleone and Cisterna in a two-pronged operation, the Allies may have made their only important objective that of seizing the Alban Hills in a concerted, armoured and infantry attack astride of the Anzio–Albano road.

Instead, the reality was that two infantry divisions dissipated their strength in a thin spread of troops over an ever-widening front. A particular illustration of this occurrence serves to demonstrate the point. It comes from the *Times* report of March 1944 which records an episode in which it names the 1st Reconnaissance Regiment as a 'thin, red line' of 172 men holding a front of two miles; my own C Squadron being of 86 men holding a front of 1,800 yards.

On 28 January 1944, the arrival of the 1st American Armoured Division came too late to be used in a thrust for the Alban Hills. It was employed in small, limited and abortive counter-attack roles.

So, can there be any blame apportioned for the lack of success of 'Shingle'? Could it be directed towards the Supreme High Command of the Allies?

The High Command was engrossed in momentous preparations for 'Operation Overlord', the D-Day landings. It was clear that 'Operation Shingle' was far from being at the head of the Command's list of priorities. Churchill and his military chiefs were enthusiastic about the plan to break the deadlock in Italy.

Roosevelt and his advisers were lukewarm. 'Shingle' became bedevilled by arguments over numbers of landing craft being made available for its execution. These wranglings ended when Prime Minister Churchill gave in to the American will. His predicament is revealed in this extract from his book, *Closing The Ring.*

Everything turned on landing craft which held for some weeks all our strategy in the tightest ligature. I did not dare to demand the necessary weight and volume for 'cat claw' (the Anzio Landing). If the extravagant demands of the military machine had been reduced, we could have flung ashore, south of the Tiber, a still larger force with full mobility. If I had asked for a three-division lift, I should not have got anything. How often in life must one be content with what one can get, still, it would be better to do the right.'

But, for the landing force, right was not done so it was of no use Winston complaining that he had hoped 'that we were hurling a wild cat on to the shore but all we got was a stranded whale'. Colourful words these which cloaked the gallantry, the endurance and sacrifice of the infantry battalions of the 1st British Infantry Division. There were heavy casualties in the dark and perilous early days of battle and in the months of trench warfare. *The History Of The First British Infantry Division* confirms the sacrifices made by compiling the following list of casualties sustained by the division in the period from January to June 1944:

	Casualties	Percentage of the Divisional Total
24th Guards Brigade (Relieved in early March by the 18th Motorized Brigade)	1,988	22.4%
2nd Infantry Brigade	2,014	22.75%
3rd Infantry Brigade	2,327	23.29%

18th Motorized Brigade (Replaced 24th Guards Brigade, March 1944)	1,019	11.5%

Therein lies praise not blame. Apparent failure in strategy gives place to both supreme sacrifice and the endurance of those who survived. Success surely lies in the indomitable spirit and *esprit de corps* of the men of Anzio both British and American, in the strength and durability of all ranks, in the high morale in the face of constant bombardment, and in the patient acceptance of the troglodyte existence below ground.

Even Kesselring underestimated the will of the men of Anzio. With a modicum of compassion, he wrote:

I constantly kept in mind the psychological effect of their situation on the staff and troops of the 6th American Corps. Penned in as they were on a notoriously unhealthy coast, it must have been damned unpleasant; our heavy artillery and the Luftwaffe with its numerous flak batteries and bombers alone saw to it that even when 'resting' their soldiers had no rest.

For the Anzio man, irrespective of whether butterfly bombs were falling by night or shells falling by day, when he was off duty, he learned to fall into sleep as if it were an impervious, impenetrable barrier to harm. By day, even though he was caught in the open by shell fire, he dropped into the nearest one of myriads of dug-outs or slit trenches and then, when the shelling had ceased, resumed his duties as if there had been no interruption.

More than that, Kesselring's description of a notorious, unhealthy coast which had taken its toll of malaria-stricken German troops, is belied by the fact that not one case of malaria was reported among the men of Anzio. Forward planning had ensured that there came ashore, with the assaulting troops, field hygiene sections of the Royal Army Medical Corps. Their task was to fill in swampy ground, treat stagnant pools and to wage war on the malaria-carrying mosquito.

A vindication of the efforts of Anzio man came from Winston

Churchill. In his book, *Closing The Ring*, he praised both the Anzio campaigners and the Allied armies attacking from the south. He wrote:

> We now know that early in January, the German High Command had intended to transfer five of their best divisions from Italy to north-west Europe.

Kesselring protested to the High Command that, if so, he would have to withdraw from Rome. But, when the Anzio Campaign was mounted, the German High Command dropped the idea. Churchill wrote of this change of enemy tactic in the following words:

> Instead of the Italian front contributing forces to north-west Europe, the reverse took place.
> We knew nothing of these changes of plan at the time, but it proves that the aggressive action of our armies in Italy and, specifically, the Anzio stroke made its full contribution towards the success of 'Overlord'.

What may not be generally known is that, once 'Overlord' began, so the reinforcements from Britain, for the British troops in Italy, ended. Every British infantry battalion was reduced to three rifle companies instead of four and so lost a quarter of its strength. In the 1st Reconnaissance Regiment, officer reinforcements came from South Africa. To the credit of General Alexander, who commanded in Italy, these reductions in manpower failed to stop his mounting of aggressive operations even though his troops were outnumbered by opposing German formations.

It was only in the Apennines, with the River Po valley within striking distance, that the Allies paused in their progress to reorganize and prepare for an all-out offensive in the spring of 1945.

It was in the winter months of 1944 that the 1st British Infantry Division found itself in the mountains, holding the Monte Grande sector facing Bologna. Its soldiers were soon to find that warfare in the wintry Apennines was demanding both physically and mentally. At heights of 2,000 metres or more, night patrolling, the manning of the outpost line and observation posts brought fatigue and discomfort. High up in the hills, the rains seemed heavier and more prolonged. Snow and mud were deeper, and mists more frequent and sudden, making life unpleasant for the dismounted trooper as he climbed and descended the forward slopes of the defence line.

Supplies were difficult to come by. Pack transport by mules was the only means of maintaining the forward squadrons. Daily supplies of ammunition and food were brought upwards – ammunition, mostly of 3-inch mortar bombs, took priority. In the case of an enemy attack, they were the only means of providing very close support for the defenders.

For the wounded, there was a horrendous journey down steep, irregular, narrow mountain tracks into the valley below. From there, stretcher-bearing Jeeps awaited to carry them along bumpy tracks and crumbling minor roads to the nearest field ambulance unit.

Sometimes, on dangerous down slopes, mules bearing panniers which held stretchers were used but, with their jolting gait and sudden petulance, it must have been a terrifying and painful experience for the wounded. The mules came to be used in this way only at the last resort when it was found that four stretcher-bearers, exercising thoughtfulness and care, made the climb down less alarming and more comfortable for the casualty.

For three months, the men of the 1st Reconnaissance Regiment showed their resilience in the vicissitudes of mountain warfare. With difficulty, disciplined and proud, they observed the common decencies. All washed and shaved regularly and although their clothing was damp and mud-stained, their weapons were kept clean and ready. Then, towards the end of their commitment on Marzolina, they were rewarded. By dint of a superb effort by the Royal Engineers, the ground floor of 17 Troop's daytime haven, the barn close to regimental headquarters, was converted into a primitive but effective shower room with, wonders upon wonders, hot water. There, only 400 yards behind the front line, men from both the regiment and the Reserve Infantry Battalion, in small groups, could further cleanse themselves.

Meanwhile, the regiment's own pioneers had constructed a canvas-screened latrine where, for the first time in months, there was a degree of privacy usually denied the front-line soldier.

So, from Paddy, the regimental commander, down to trooper, morale was high and spirit unbroken. In high regard of all in 1st Reconnaissance Regiment - the fallen, those who have by this time have died and those who remain - I pay this last tribute. I salute its soldiers in the popular Christian names of the era in which they were born. Well done, I say, to the Tommys, the Freddys and the Harrys: to the Joes, the Jimmys and the Johnnys and to the Georges, Bills and Arthurs. My memories of your comradeship, durability and courage will remain.